Under the Tree

Under the Tree

THE TOYS AND TREATS THAT MADE CHRISTMAS SPECIAL, 1930–1970

SUSAN WAGGONER

STEWART, TABORI & CHANG
NEW YORK

Published in 2007 by Stewart, Tabori & Chang
An imprint of Harry N. Abrams, Inc.

Library of Congress Cataloging-in-Publication Data:

Waggoner, Susan.
  Under the tree : the toys and treats that made Christmas special, 1930-1970 / Susan Waggoner.
     p. cm.
  ISBN-13: 978-1-58479-641-1
  ISBN-10: 1-58479-641-3
  1. Christmas—United States—History—20th century. 2. Toys—United States—History—20th century. 3. Gifts—United States—History—20th century. I. Title.

GT4985.W35 2007
394.2663—dc22

2007006613

Editor: Dervla Kelly
Designer: Kay Schuckhart/Blond on Pond
Production Manager: Tina Cameron

The text of this book was composed in Adobe Caslon, Valentina Joy, and Bauer Bodoni Black.

Printed and bound in China
10 9 8 7 6 5 4 3 2 1

HNA
harry n. abrams, inc.
a subsidiary of La Martinière Groupe

115 West 18th Street
New York, NY 10011
www.hnabooks.com

CONTENTS

AMF products ARE BETTER...by design
AMERICAN MACHINE & FOUNDRY COMPANY

Roadmaster

A Sleigh Full of Toys, and St. Nicholas Too

Christmas—such a bonanza of toys, treats, and time away from school you'd think it was invented by kids themselves. It wasn't, though, and the Christmas we know today, complete with presents piled beneath a tree, comes to us across centuries of evolution.

Ancient Romans observed the Saturnalia, a weeklong festival honoring the winter solstice. Just as they do today, children received gifts from their parents, enjoyed a holiday from school, attended family parties, and were given uncommon access to sweets. Early Christians won converts by merging the Saturnalia's most popular features with the new holiday, Christmas.

Ultimately, however, Christmas was a far more solemn holiday than the Saturnalia, and the toy extravaganza we know today didn't really get its start until the nineteenth century. The change began in 1823 with Clement Moore's poem, "A Visit from St. Nicholas," with its famous opening line, "'Twas the night before Christmas." This poem replaced the image of the thin, somewhat forbidding European Santa Claus with a cheerful, robust American Santa, a rotund elf with twinkling eyes and merry dimples. And did we mention his sleigh full of toys? The European St. Nick dispensed charity to the poor, but the American version gave toys to good children everywhere.

Spending—especially on children—was not a display of sinful excess but a demonstration of the Christmas spirit itself. Germany became the toy-making capital of the world, with whole families working at home to turn out toys for children throughout Europe and America. As one traveler observed, in some cities almost every house was a toy factory.

Marvelous as the German toys were, importation costs kept them relatively expensive—until retailer Frank Woolworth taught the German toy-makers to mass-produce goods and ship them to his warehouses for packaging and distribution. His method would become a huge success, and countless children had merry Christmases because Woolworth's stores featured products that almost every family could afford.

An even bigger change came with World War I, which temporarily halted most international trade. From that time on, an ever-growing variety of toys were produced in America. Interruptions like the Depression and World War II turned out to be just that—interruptions. In fact, World War II was ultimately a catalyst, as couples who had been separated for four long, dangerous years wanted nothing more than to settle down, have children, and do Christmas on a bigger scale than ever before.

The last ingredient in the toy extravaganza was television. No longer did manufacturers have to persuade Mom and Dad of a toy's potential; through TV, they could go directly to the consumer. Children who saw the Mr. Potato Head commercial understood at once what a desirable thing it would be to stick eyes, ears, noses, and glasses on a familiar vegetable. They clamored for the toy, and sales went through the roof. It didn't take long for other manufacturers to follow suit.

It's become fashionable, over the years, to insist that Christmas is cluttered with too many toys, that our children are spoiled and should learn to live with less. But who among us doesn't harbor the memory of a magical Christmas and a special toy?

Ask yourself, can this be a *bad* thing? We don't think so.

CHRISTMAS PAST AND PRESENTS

1924: Money spent annually on toys in America: $100 million

1936: Annual income of U.S. Christmas tree industry: $10 million

1940: Annual spending on Christmas cards in the U.S.: $30 million

1945: Money spent annually on toys in America: $200 million

1960: Cost to gift wrap the nation's presents: $150 million

1962: Least expensive of the 12,000 toys sold at FAO Schwarz in New York: a 15 cent whistle; most expensive: a four-room puppet theater, fully furnished, $2,000

1968: Money spent annually on toys in America: $2 billion

2005: Money spent annually on toys in America: $22.9 billion

Oh! You Beautiful Doll

Her presence under the tree is as ubiquitous as the electric train—fitting, since she's older than the train or even the tree itself. In fact, she's one of the oldest toys on earth, dating back more than four thousand years. Despite her age, she's been relatively immune to modification, and a little girl from ancient Egypt, catapulted into Macy's, would know what Barbie was all about in a flash.

THE WORLD'S MOST POPULAR TOY

Dolls and human figures are among the oldest of all toys, but it wasn't until the tail end of the nineteenth century that methods of mass production and improved world trade made store bought dolls truly affordable. Doll manufacturers like Ideal, Madame Alexander, and Vogue all got their start in the early decades of the twentieth century, and sales clicked

along nicely—until October 1929 brought the start of the Great Depression. Then, just like the railroads, Standard Oil, and U.S. Steel, doll-makers suffered plummeting sales. Even the It doll of the 1920s, the inexpensive Kewpie doll, gathered dust on store shelves. Instead of getting a new doll for Christmas in the early 1930s, a little girl might get new clothes, usually made by Mother, for a doll that had been new in 1928.

Some doll makers responded to hard times by creating dolls that were must-have items. Effenbee brought out their DyDee doll, a young miss who drank from a bottle, wet her diapers, and blew bubbles. Not to be outdone, Ideal brought out Betsy Wetsy. Betsy's similarity to DyDee resulted in a lawsuit, and a legal ruling that drinking and wetting could not be patented.

LITTLE MISS MERCHANDISE

As if in answer to the toy industry's prayers, a little girl born just eighteen months before the stock market crash became the biggest thing in the history of the movies. Her name was Shirley Temple. She was on the cover of *Time* in April 1936, just a few days after her eighth birthday. Her movies, turned out at the rate of more than four a year, earned her a salary of $75,000—an annual salary of about $4.4 million at

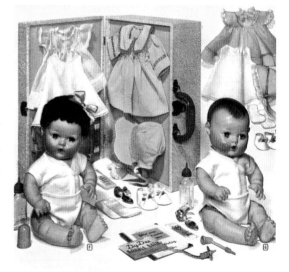

Effanbee's Rubber "Dy-dee" Dolls

today's rates. Few people received as much mail (nearly four thousand letters a week), and only President Roosevelt and King Edward VIII were more photographed.

Throughout the hardscrabble days of the Depression, Americans saw in her roles much of what they looked for in themselves and their country, a combination of sweetness and pluck that allowed her to overcome adversity with optimism intact. Not only did children go to Shirley Temple movies, adults went as well, and they bought figurines and postcards and dishes with her picture on them. When it came to sheet music sales, Temple's face on the cover was almost as valuable as Bing Crosby's.

It's likely that no human image, before or since, has appeared on so many toys, under so many Christmas trees, for so many years. Ideal produced the first Shirley Temple doll in 1934, and soon there were dozens, in every size imaginable, made of everything from soft cloth to vinyl to porcelain, dressed in costumes from movies like *Little Miss Marker*, *Captain January*, and *Heidi*.

Besides dolls, there were Shirley Temple paper dolls, books, coloring books, and activity books, along with Shirley Temple doll carriages and ironing boards. There were embroidery kits, pen and pencil sets, games, jewelry sets, tea sets and toiletries. For the well-accessorized young fan, there were Shirley Temple barrettes, hair ribbons, and pocket books: in fact, there was an entire line of clothes, from underwear to dresses to overcoats.

Long after the pint-sized star grew up, items bearing her name continued to sell, and Shirley Temple dolls were made for little girls until well into the 1970s.

People in the news also helped another doll maker, Bertha Alexander, better known as Madame Alexander. The Alexander Doll company had been in business since 1923, but the event that put the company on the map was the birth of the Dionne quintuplets in Canada in 1934. The Dionne sisters, the first quintuplets ever to survive, caused an international stir. People were fascinated by them, so much so that a theme park, Quintland, eventually sprang up around the government-sponsored facility where they lived. Madame Alexander produced dolls representing the five little girls, and their enormous popularity helped push doll sales to a record twenty-two million dollars in 1936.

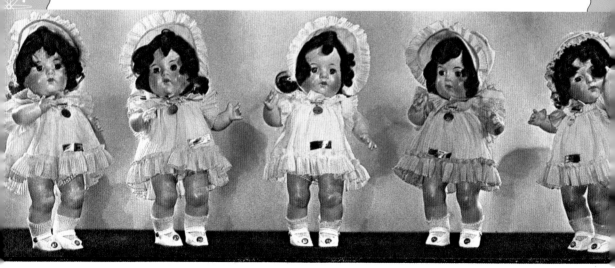

MADAME ALEXANDER'S QUINTUPLETS WILL PROBABLY RANK THIRD IN SALES THIS SEASON . . .

In the 1940s, war production put an end to the unemployment and low wages of the Depression. Unfortunately for children, rubber and many other materials that had previously gone into making dolls were redirected toward the war effort. Cloth dolls were an acceptable alternative, and if they couldn't be *better* than the prewar dolls with elastic-jointed limbs and eyes that opened and closed, they could at least be *bigger*. Dolls big enough to dance with and dress in real clothes became popular, and remained so well into the 1950s.

If you grew up in the 1950s and feel especially nostalgic about your dolls, it isn't just the glow of childhood speaking. The 1950s and early '60s really were the golden age of dolls. In 1951, *Time* magazine reported that Rich's, a popular Atlanta department store, had allocated fifteen percent more room to its toy department than the previous Christmas and opened a special department just for doll clothes.

Dolls didn't just say "Mama" or "Papa," they also smiled, clapped their hands, and danced on the toes of their pink ballet shoes. And the best part? Little girls didn't have to choose just one or two dolls. In millions of bedrooms, in thousands of newly built suburbs, they assembled families and cities and communities of dolls—baby dolls in bassinettes and toddler dolls in strollers, dolls that came with their own beauty parlors, dolls whose hair grew at the turn of a key, and storybook dolls that did nothing but lie on satin bedspreads with their full skirts blooming around them. Here are just a few of the dolls that made a splash in the postwar decades.

They'll Kneel, Sit, and Pose!

See All The Things We Can Do!

DOLLS BY THE DECADE

1920s: Popular dolls include Kewpie dolls, Raggedy Ann and Andy, Indian dolls, and dolls that can talk

1933: Effanbee's DyDee doll, the first doll to drink, wet, and blow bubbles. DyDee charms children and dismays grown-ups unlucky enough to hold her

1934: The first of many Shirley Temple dolls is made by Ideal

1934: Ideal introduces Betsy Wetsy, who becomes one of the most popular dolls of the twentieth century. Who knew damp drawers could take you so far?

1935: Dionne Quintuplet dolls, by Madame Alexander

1937: Tie-in time: Knickerbocker Toy Co. makes a Snow White doll, along with all seven dwarves, to capitalize on Disney's hit movie.

1939: Little Lulu dolls, by Knickerbocker

1949: Nina Ballerina, by Madame Alexander

1950: Tiny Tears, by American Character

1951: Vogue's Ginny, a little girl with a bean-shaped body, is an eight-inch sensation.

1952: Madame Alexander presents Cynthia, an African American girl dressed for a party.

1953: Wendy, Madame Alexander's counterpart to Vogue's Ginny, arrives.

1953: Winnie Walker and Binnie Walker, by Madame Alexander, debut with Cissy's beautiful face, but lack her curves and high-heeled feet.

1955: Cissy, the first full-figured, high-heeled fashion doll, is released by Madame Alexander.

1956: Miss Revlon, from Ideal. Like Cissy, Miss Revlon has a grown-up body and wears sophisticated clothes and high heels.

1957: Jill, Ginny's older, shapelier sister, by Vogue

1957: American Character produces a Betsy McCall doll that, at eight inches, is four inches shorter than Ideal's 1952 version.

1958: Little Miss Revlon, by Ideal

1958: Toni, by American Character, joins the trend toward full-figured dolls.

1958: Pitiful Pearl, a winsomely homely little girl doll, demonstrates the value of just being yourself.

4^{99}

1959: Clad only in a black-and-white striped swimsuit, heels, and sunglasses, Barbie starts her climb to the top of the toy world.

1960: Chatty Cathy, from Mattel, proves that you don't have to wear heels and a garter belt to succeed in the doll world.

1961: Kissy, from Ideal. Press her arms together and she kisses.

1962: Ideal's Tammy—"The Doll You Love To Dress"—is offered as a teenage alternative to Barbie. Like the wholesome girl who volunteers for everything, she never quite makes it into the in crowd.

1963: Tammy's little sister, Pepper, is brought out by Ideal.

1964: Suzy Homemaker, from Topper Toys, makes her debut, bringing a whole line of chic aqua appliances with her, as well as her own beauty parlor.

1964: Tressy, the doll with "growing" hair, debuts from American Character, along with her more obscure counterpart, Mary Make-up.

1966: Ranging from just two and three quarters to four inches tall, Mattel's Liddle Kiddles spark a craze for pocket-sized dolls.

BETSY WETSY AND TINY TEARS

Babies and toddlers were everywhere in the years after the war, so it's no surprise that they dominated the doll shelves as well. A baby doll was just the ticket for a girl who had a little brother or sister at home. Betsy Wetsy, originally issued by Ideal in 1934, enjoyed many modifications over the years. She was popular enough to sell well in several sizes in the 1940s and was one of the first big-name dolls to come in an African American

version. She experienced a resurgence of popularity in the early 1950s and was able to hold her own with baby dolls many years her junior.

Tiny Tears, the best-selling baby doll of the 1950s, made her debut, appropriately, at a launch party held at the Stork Club at the start of the decade. Dressed entirely in pink and white, with an embroidered onesie that became her signature outfit and a patented mechanism that funneled tears from the corners of her eyes, Tiny Tears was an appealing doll that wasn't all that much different from predecessors like Betsy Wetsy and the DyDee doll. Yet she quickly took the lead in the baby doll world by using another new toy, television, to her advantage. Commercials, some starring a very young (and still unknown)

> *We have two factories, but we can't make 'em fast enough for the demand. We have no stock on the floor.*
>
> — American Character Dolls executive, speaking of Tiny Tears

Patty Duke, aired on popular children's shows, and one of the shows, *Ding-Dong School*, was especially instrumental in boosting sales. Hosted by the mumsy-looking Miss Frances, the show consciously tried to provide high-quality, learning-oriented programming to children. Adults trusted Miss Frances, and if a doll met with her approval, it was definitely good enough for Santa to bring.

DOLLS TO GROW ON: GINNY AND WENDY

It wasn't long until the bumper crop of babies born after World War II began to grow up. Toddlers turned into little girls ready for their first day at school, and at each stage there

was a doll that looked a lot like they did. At the start of the 1950s, the Vogue Doll company, created by Jennie Graves, employed fifty full-time workers and up to two hundred freelance seamstresses, and had a sales volume of about $239,000 a year. Responding to a dip in sales, Graves created a new doll, a little girl just eight inches tall. The prototype sold so well that the line went into full production, and Ginny, named after the creator's daughter, appeared on toy shelves in 1951. Her hard plastic body wasn't the soft, cuddly baby doll–type girls were used to; it was a body they saw every day when they looked in the mirror. Ginny's sweet face, slightly pudgy tummy, and sturdy legs made for a true-to life replica of a young miss of the 1950s, and girls fell instantly in love. Ginny dressed in clothes that resembled her owner's as well—navy blue coats with white collars, cuffs, and straw hat; pink ginham sundresses; pleated plaid skirts with knit sweaters and matching red berets. By 1953, Vogue's sales exceeded two million dollars a year, and Ginny was a permanent fixture on the doll scene.

Girls flip over the new "mod" London look. So does our new Francie.™

Francie is Barbie's fifteen year old cousin. Like most girls her age, she loves to wear stripes, paisley prints, London lace, and granny gowns.

(And our bending leg Francie even has real eyelashes.)

Francie is very real to girls who'll be fifteen someday, too. That's why she's so much fun.

Francie

Ginny's arrival sparked a passion for eight-inch girl dolls, and soon every company had its own version. One of the best known and most enduring was Wendy, by Madame Alexander. Like Ginny, Wendy's popularity lay in the basics: She was a sweet-faced, well-made doll whose wardrobe was composed of intricately made outfits bound to capture a girl's attention. And if you couldn't decide what to dress Wendy in, no matter—she became the foundation doll for all sorts of Madame Alexander themed collections. There were holiday dolls dressed for Valentine's Day, Christmas, and Easter; dolls from many lands; dolls for special occasions such as graduation, First Communion, or being a flower girl; and storybook dolls such as *Little Women's* Meg, Jo, Beth, and Amy, along with their mother, Marmee.

TO FASHION OR NOT TO FASHION: DOLLS THAT BROKE THE BARRIER

It was out there, looming like a gigantic meteor most parents didn't want to think about. Little girls were getting older. And more sophisticated. In the 1930s, ten-year-olds read

The Bobbsey Twins and wanted roller skates for Christmas. In the 1950s, they watched *American Bandstand* and had, for the most part, outgrown their dolls. There had always been grown-up dolls, of course—bride dolls mostly, along with ballerinas, nurses, and nuns. In 1953, Madame Alexander brought out Winnie and Binnie Walker, virtually identical dolls with a breathtakingly beautiful face and fashion-forward wardrobe. They were clearly meant to be grown-ups, but like all the dolls that had gone before them, they had undeveloped bodies and flat feet.

To make her dreams come true . . . famous Mme. Alexander dolls, none finer made

Breaking the curvature barrier was no easy matter. When Madame Alexander finally did it in 1955 with Cissy, it was after a lot of deliberation. Creator Beatrice Alexander later confessed that, afraid of offending everyone from the DAR to the Junior League to the toy makers of America, she held the doll back for three years. Apparently with good cause. Dressed in a lace camisole, nylon stockings, and mules, Cissy was quickly surrounded by toy fair attendees who "ogled her ecstatically." Yet the Alexander name had enormous credibility and a track record of excellence, and buyers were eventually persuaded that the doll was a serious attempt to introduce young girls to fashion.

Because Cissy was a relatively expensive doll, not every girl got her. But almost every girl got the message—this doll was grown up, and would help demystify the puzzling transition to womanhood. It wasn't long until other equally grown-up dolls came along, from a variety of manufacturers and in a variety sizes, at prices so varied most little girls soon had one.

One of the first, debuting in 1956, was Ideal's Miss Revlon, often spotted wearing earrings and carrying a small handbag emblazoned with the Revlon logo. Like Cissy, she wore high heels and had any number of costumes worthy of a sophisticated lifestyle, from debutante gowns to peignoir sets to a "TV lounging outfit" complete with cat-eye glasses. A year later Vogue brought

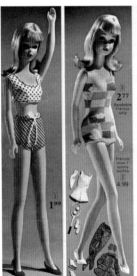

If you'd like a doll with the Young London Look,

Meet Francie,

Barbie's cousin—she's back from England, and has brought all those Carnaby Street styles with her

[1] FRANCIE DOLL. She's back from abroad and ready to get back into the swing of things. Dressed in a pretty two-piece cotton bathing suit—colorful polka dot top, checked shorts. High heels complement her outfit. Smooth, flesh-toned plastic skin and shoulder-length rooted hair. 11¼ in. tall. Select from 10 more outfits shown below. From Japan.
X 921-0650 A—Shipping weight 7 oz. 1.99

[2] BENDABLE FRANCIE DOLL. Barbie's cousin has lifelike legs that bend—she's ready to do all those British dances! Little girls love her rooted shoulder-length hairdo and her realistic rooted eyelashes. Smooth, flesh-toned plastic body. Francie wears a bright cotton print one-piece swimsuit, high heels. Comes with her own eyelash brush. 11¼ in. tall. Dress her up in outfits shown below, and take her wherever you go. From Japan.
X 921-0568 A—Shipping weight 7 oz. 2.77

[3] FRANCIE'S SPORTIN' SET. Stylish bendable Francie comes with two sporty outfits. Skating outfit with skating skirt, leotards, sweater, skates, and mittens. Tennis ensemble comes with tennis dress, racket, and balls She wears a one-piece swimsuit and shoes. Francie even has her own eyelash brush. Bendable legs, rooted eyelashes and shoulder-length hairdo. Flesh-toned plastic doll is 11¼ in. tall. Wire stand included.
X 921-9825 A—Shipping weight 1 lb. 4 oz. 4.99

10 more kicky outfits for every occasion

[4] GAD-ABOUT COSTUME. Blue-green Jacquard cotton knit sweater, matching hose. Cotton-knit shirt, hat. Sunglasses, shoes, hanger included.*
X 921-0576 A—Shpg. wt. 3 oz. 1.44

[5] TUCKERED OUT. White cotton nightie with blue gingham check trim, matching cap and sleeping bootees. Mirror, rollers, hairbrush, comb, hanger included.*
X 921-0584 A—Shpg. wt. 3 oz. 1.44

[6] RAINY-DAY OUTFIT. Red and white polka-dotted plastic raincoat with zippered pockets and yellow lining. Red kerchief, red rain boots, and hanger included*.
X 921-0592 A—Shpg. wt. 3 oz. 1.44

[7] CLAM DIGGERS. Orange and yellow vinyl plastic jacket, hat. Yellow cotton-knit top, orange stretch pants, yellow shoes. Orange sunglasses, hanger.*
X 921-0618 A—Shpg. wt. 4 oz. 2.19

[8] FIRST FORMAL. Gown has blue crepe sleeveless bodice, embroidered organdy overskirt, taffeta underskirt. Orange cape. Gloves, shoes, hanger.*
X 921-0669 A—Shpg. wt. 4 oz. 2.19

[9] SHOPPIN' SPREE. Pink and white cotton tweed coat, matching purse. Pink and white crepe sleeveless dress. Short white gloves, pink shoes, hanger included.*
X 921-0683 A—Shpg. wt. 4 oz. 2.19

[10] IT'S A DATE. Turquoise and blue-colored cotton dress with polka dots and stripes. Toilette bow on high waist, white collar, cuffs. Hose, shoes.*
X 921-0725 A—Shpg. wt. 3 oz. 1.44

[11] DANCE PARTY. Pink crepe dress with white lace collar and sleeves, lace bonnet. White nylon tricot hose and slip. Flat shoes. Record player, records, portrait, spoon, napkin and hanger included.*
X 921-0733 A—Shpg. wt. 4 oz. 2.19

[12] CHECKMATES. Red, white, blue houndstooth cotton checked jacket, pleated skirt. White sleeveless blouse. Red vinyl plastic purse and shoes. Hanger.*
X 921-0758 A—Shpg. wt. 4 oz. 2.19

[13] FIRST THINGS FIRST. Lace-edged printed tricot petticoats, garter belt, panty, half-slip. Nylon lace hose, hanger.*
X 921-0741 A—Shpg. wt. 3 oz. 1.44

*From Japan. Doll not included.

10 New Outfits are "Simply Fab"
Choose Francie's wardrobe from a variety of stripes, checks, polka dots

B 2.82

Miss Toni and her wave kit

out Jill, Ginny's big sister. Jill introduced another new size into the fashion lineup, standing ten and a half inches in her high-heeled feet. The size made for popular, affordable dolls and outfits, and Jill was joined by a Little Miss Revlon in the same size in 1958.

American Character's hit fashion doll of the era was Toni, also introduced in 1958. Not to be confused with Ideal's Toni, a girl doll of the early 1950s whose hair could be permed and styled, American Character's Toni was a grown-up fashion doll whose outfits bore such alluring names as "Suburbanite," "American Beauty Formal," and "High Society." Toni came in four sizes, ranging from ten and half to twenty-five inches, and had rooted hair that could be set and waved.

The passion for fashion dolls that started with Cissy in 1955 was still raging as the decade drew to a close, and the time would soon be just right for one more doll to come along and take the world by storm.

BARBIE CHANGES THE WORLD

She's better than you. And curvier. With cooler clothes, a newer car, and more career options. Her boyfriend is always available but never demanding, and her friends don't seem to mind letting her take center stage. And, although she has a first, middle, and last name, the whole world knows her by the first alone—Barbie.

Barbie was invented by Ruth Handler, who got the idea for a glamorous adult doll with a huge wardrobe by watching her daughter play with paper dolls. Introduced by Mattel at the annual Toy Fair in 1959, Barbie's future was far from certain. Her va-va-voom figure, black mascara, uptilted eyes, and arched eyebrows were like nothing the toy world had ever seen. While adults debated whether or not Barbie was too grown up, little girls clamored for her. Both Barbie and her detailed outfits were a smash hit and dominated Christmas lists from 1960 on.

Where adults saw a disturbingly adult doll, little girls saw something else: accessories and an eye for detail. Barbie's clothes were intricately tailored, with real zippers, miniature buttons, matching belts, and ornamental trims. The same outfit in human size, hanging on a rack at Saks, would not have been out of place. Best of all, the outfits came with fascinating assortments of miniature accessories. Her barbecue outfit included a chef's toque, rolling pin, three-piece utensil set, and red plaid potholder. Her yellow terrycloth bathrobe came with a beribboned blue shower cap, bath sponge, towel, washcloth, talcum box and

BARBIE BASICS

NAME: Barbie Millicent Roberts

APPROXIMATE LIFE-SIZE EQUIVALENT DIMENSIONS, IN INCHES: 39-21-33

HOMETOWN: Willow, Wisconsin

PARENTS: Robert and Margaret Roberts

SISTER: Skipper

1960s FRIENDS: Midge, Francie, Stacey, Christie

BOYFRIEND: Ken Carson

CAREER: Teen fashion model

FAVORITE INDULGENCE: Clothes—since her debut, well over a hundred million yards of fabric have gone into her wardrobe, making Mattel America's fourth-largest manufacturer of women's garments.

FANS: Literally millions; over 90% of American girls from the baby boom on puff, and tiny bar of plastic soap.

In time Barbie acquired friends, a little sister, a boyfriend, a car, and numerous dream houses. She changed the doll world forever and taught millions of little girls that stylish, well-tailored clothes, along with the right accessories, are almost always a good investment. A few other dolls tried to compete with Barbie, most notably Tammy, a more wholesome, teenagerish fashion doll; Tressy, whose hair grew or shortened with the turn of a key; and Suzy Homemaker, who had an alluring set of appliances. They were all good dolls but no match for Barbie's charm and sophistication.

In the end, despite her lush proportions and glamorous image, Barbie never coasted on good looks. From teenage fashion model she branched out to numerous other careers, trying her hand at everything a little girl might dream of being. As for the little girls who played with her, they've grown up to achieve some pretty remarkable things themselves.

You can color-style Barbie®

HI! I'M CHATTY CATHY

Just when parents feared fashion dolls were making little girl dolls a thing of the past, along came toothy, freckle-faced, Chatty Cathy. And, ironically, she was made by the very same

folks who created Barbie. They knew what they were up to because, like Barbie, Cathy was an instant hit. She had something no other doll had—dialogue. Sure, there had been dolls that cried before, and dolls that said "mama," but Chatty Cathy spoke whole phrases that played, at random, when you pulled the string at the back of her neck. Included in the original eleven phrases were things any ultra-polite four-year-old might say, such as "Please give me a kiss," "Tell me a story," "Will you play with me?" and "Please take me with you." Later, her vocabulary expanded to eighteen phrases, and in versions for foreign markets

she spoke Spanish, German, or French. When it came to vocal coaching, Chatty Cathy had the best—her original voice belonged to June Foray, who was also the voice of Rocky the Flying Squirrel, Natasha Fatale, and Nell Fenwick in Jay Ward cartoons, and the voice of Talking Tina in "The Living Doll," a *Twilight Zone* episode undoubtedly inspired by the Chatty Cathy phenomenon. When Chatty Cathy was reissued in the late 1960s, Maureen McCormack—better known as Marcia from *The Brady Bunch*—supplied the voice. The original Chatty Cathy was wildly popular and remained in constant production well into the 1960s, making her second only to Barbie as the most beloved doll of the decade.

SOMETHING FOR THE BOYS

Of course there were dolls for boys. Raggedy Ann's companion, Raggedy Andy, dates back to World War I. In the 1930s, Edgar Bergen popularized the art of ventriloquism, and ventriloquist dolls based on wisecracking, monocle-wearing Charlie McCarthy were sold to a predominantly male market. So were two other ventriloquist dolls, TV characters Jerry Mahoney and Knucklehead Smith, creations of Paul Winchell. Another 1950s TV offering, The *Howdy Doody Show*, featured a cast of marionettes that appealed to boys. In addition to freckle-faced Howdy himself, residents of Doodyville included Howdy's friend Dilly

(38) DENNIS THE MEN-ACE DOLL. This lovable, irresistible character has been faithfully reproduced into an adorable 17" doll with vinyl head, latex body and dressed characteristically in snappy denim overalls and striped "T" shirt. All ages. (17) $3.98

Dally, Mayor Phineas T. Bluster, and a mythical beast called the Flub-a-dub. Another success for boys was Dennis the Menace, who came in several sizes and versions. Neither

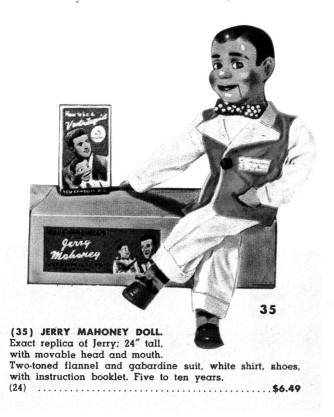

(35) JERRY MAHONEY DOLL.
Exact replica of Jerry; 24" tall, with movable head and mouth. Two-toned flannel and gabardine suit, white shirt, shoes, with instruction booklet. Five to ten years. (24) $6.49

a marionette nor a ventriloquist's dummy, Dennis's mischievous, snips-and-snails personality overcame any notion that he might be a sissy. But, ironically, the most doll-like toys for boys, the cowboy action figures of the 1950s and the 1960s' G.I. Joe, were *never* referred to as "dolls," even in jest. So, throwing logic to the winds, We've bowed to tradition and put them in the Small World chapter, on page 77.

SO TWO-DIMENSIONAL: PAPER DOLLS

With a worldwide Depression on and families both urban and rural struggling to put food on the table, the dolls of Christmases past became mere wishes for many little girls. Fortunately, a substitute was already at hand, and paper dolls became one of the most popular gifts of the 1930s.

By no means new, paper dolls date back to the eighteenth century, when they were considered luxuries due to the expense of paper and the fact that most were hand-painted. One hundred years later, they were being made in the U.S. as well as Europe. The most affordable sets were printed in black ink on white paper, leaving the user to color the outfits herself. The sets came in paper envelopes or small boxes, and the featured doll was almost always an idealized version of the user—a dimpled little girl between the ages of four and eight, living an ordinary life with an ordinary family somewhere in Smalltown, USA.

In the 1930s, that began to change. Aware that paper dolls might be the only doll a little girl might get for Christmas, manufacturers looked for new ways to make them glamorous and appealing. And where better to look than to the movies? The most bankable star of the day was also, fortuitously, a little girl. Shirley Temple, the country's number-one box-office star, was a perfect blend of the familiar and the glamorous, little-girl innocence and Hollywood stardust. The dolls, which came with a lavish assortment of dresses and accessories, made little girls forget that times were hard and paper was second best. And it taught manufacturers an important lesson: Hollywood sells. Gradually, little-girl dolls dropped to the background and celebrity and movie-star dolls took center stage.

Rita Hayworth, Claudette Colbert, Debbie Reynolds, Piper Laurie, and Elizabeth Taylor were all paper dolls, as were singer Patti Page, figure skater Sonja Henie, and swimmer Esther Williams.

In the decades after World War II, paper dolls became even more affordable, selling for just a fraction of their previous price. No longer expensive enough to be a main gift, they remained popular as stocking stuffers, and most little girls had numerous sets. In addition to movie stars and athletes, TV personalities like Annette Funicello and Patty Duke joined the paper-doll parade, along with sets that celebrated the girl herself, looking ahead to such all-important life events as proms, weddings, being an airline stewardess, and dancing the lead role in Swan Lake.

In an odd twist of fate, paper dolls played a role in their own undoing. It was watching her daughter dress a paper doll in various elaborate, accessorized outfits that gave Ruth Handler the idea that a real doll, similarly adult and just as lavishly accoutered, would appeal to little girls. It did, and Handler's doll Barbie is commonly credited with bringing the golden age of paper dolls to a close.

SANTA'S SHOPPING LIST

Effanbee doll (21 ½ inches tall), in sheer black negligee, bra, lace-trimmed panties, and blue satin mules with kitten heels, 1944: $8.50

Betsy Wetsy (16 inches tall), 1947: $8.79; layette of lace-trimmed dress, bonnet, underwear, diapers, powder puff, plate, and spoon, 1947: $1.98

Ginny, in underwear, 1951: $1.98; outfits, 1951: $1 to $2.98

Tiny Tears doll, with layette, 1954: $9.95

Ballerina doll who goes en pointe when you press her hand, 1955: $9.95

Ensemble of three dresses, coat, hat, and tam, for a doll called "Miss Chubby," 1956: $2.98

Natalie Wood Paper Dolls, in folder, 1957: $.25

Toni (20 inches tall), in "Sunday Best" outfit of fitted pink net and satin dress, straw hat, heels, stockings, and purse, 1959: $11.98

Barbie, in black and white striped swimsuit, heels, and sunglasses, 1959: $3

Barbie's "Friday Night Date" outfit — powder blue corduroy jumper over white underdress, with high heels, beverage tray, and two soft drinks, 1960: $2.50

Chatty Cathy, in blue gingham dress, white eyelet blouse, blue velveteen shoes, and blue hair ribbon, 1960: $18

Kiddles, 1967: 3 for $4.98

Rolling Stock:

MODEL TRAINS, TOY TRUCKS & MORE

Just as tin soldiers were favored boys' toys of earlier centuries, so things on wheels—from trains to tanks to race cars—were favorites of the twentieth. Not that girls didn't play with model trains, cars, and even trucks, but never quite with the passion and commitment that their brothers did: Just ask any parent who ever tried to pry a new toy truck from the arms of a sleepy boy in the wee hours of Christmas night.

For many, trains remain the ultimate Christmas toy, so much a part of the season they've almost become decorations in themselves. The first model trains came from Europe, were made of wood or metal, and relied on a wind-up mechanism. By the 1890s, tracks were added, and the fact that engines ran only a short distance before rewinding was needed didn't diminish enthusiasm in the least.

In America, a seven-year old named Joshua Lionel Cowen was so enamored of real trains that he whittled a miniature one out of wood and fitted it with a tiny steam engine. Thirteen years later, he used a motor from a fan to make an electric version that ran on a circular brass track. A New York novelty store used the set for a window display and found themselves knee-deep in customers who wanted a train of their own. The young man obliged and officially went into the train business, using his own middle name—Lionel—for his fledgling company. Formed in 1900, the company sold more than a million electric train sets over the next two decades.

During the first few decades, model trains advanced rapidly, becoming more detailed and authentic. Transformers and switching systems allowed the child to control train speed and run more than one train at a time. Accessories like tunnels, stations, freight depots, trees, lamp posts, and gated crossings also appeared on the shelves.

Lionel, especially, positioned the train as the holiday gift to get, with beautifully illustrated annual catalogs and ads that proclaimed, "Everybody is happy when it's a Lionel

LIONEL TRAINS
REAL SMOKE — REAL WHISTLE

Set No. 1500 does not include MAGNE-TRACTION

1500

Ask for the new
Lionel Catalog

THE TOY OF THE CENTURY
TRAIN TIMELINE

Mid-1800s: Toy trains made of wood or metal

1900: First Lionel trains marketed

1915: Hornby, of England, begins making wind-up model trains.

1920s: Elaborately detailed accessories such as trees, stations, and bridges become an important part of model railroading

1925: Hornby's first electric trains delight children throughout the U.K.

1935: Steam whistle feature added to Lionel trains

1941-1945: Most manufacturers limit or cease production for the duration of the war, either due to metal shortages or to convert to war work.

1946: Smoke feature added to Lionel engines

1950s: The peak of model train mania. In 1955, Lionel is America's largest toy company, with two thousand employees and annual sales of about thirty-three million dollars.

1957: In an effort to appeal to girls, Lionel markets a set with a pink engine and cars in lavender, butter yellow, and pale blue.

1972: In Germany, Märklin creates the smallest trains ever, Z-gauge, 1:220 scale.

Train Christmas." Not that it took much persuasion. From their first appearance on the market, trains topped the wish list of vast numbers of American children—not to mention a growing number of dads.

Yet there were many obstacles between wish list and reality. First of all, you had to have electricity, and while most cities had power by the end of the 1920s, an enormous number of areas outside city limits did not.

Then there was the Depression. Trains were among the most expensive toys, and many people simply could not afford them. In 1937, Lionel's new and much-coveted Hudson locomotive set cost almost as much as a refrigerator. It did not sell well, but a wind-up handcar manned by Minnie and Mickey Mouse was a runaway hit. Things took a turn for the better at the end of the Depression. Europe's war put America back to

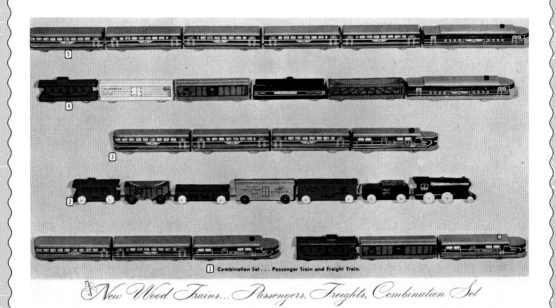

New Wood Trains... Passengers, Freights, Combination Set

work, and Lionel's 1939 catalog was a mouth-watering, beautifully illustrated extravaganza offering more than four hundred pieces of equipment.

Unfortunately, the good times were short-lived and America soon entered the war. In addition to metal and manpower shortages, many factory lines—including those that made toys—were converted for war work. Toy companies did their best to please disappointed boys, offering trains of balsa wood or heavy cardboard, but it just wasn't the same. Looking to the future, Lionel urged boys to start planning the systems they would build when their dads came back from overseas. Those who had the foresight to preorder bought up everything the manufacturers could produce. When a woman who'd ordered a $49.50 train a year in advance picked it up at the store, another customer promptly offered her $80 for it.

It wasn't really until the postwar years—almost half a century after model trains first graced Christmas windows—that wishes finally became a reality. Once they did, everyone seemed determined to make up for lost time. Trains were more appealing than ever, with details like smoke that puffed from smokestacks and a Santa Fe diesel in silver, red, and yellow that became one of the best-selling engines of all time. Little boys who, during the Depression, had never gotten the train of their dreams made sure their sons did and joined them in what quickly became one of the country's leading hobbies. And a new feature in American homes—the addition of a recreation room or finished basement—made it possible to create large, permanent layouts. Lionel even sponsored its own television show, hosted by Joe DiMaggio. At one point, there was more rolling stock on O-gauge tracks in suburbia than on actual rails. And that was just the problem. As real trains began to lose their glamour, so did their toy counterparts. New toys competed for attention. But still, who can resist the sight of a mini train speeding along though forests of tiny trees and oh-so-real-looking towns?

SANTA'S SHOPPING LIST

Original Lionel train set, with brass track, circa 1900: $6

Lionel wind-up handcar with Minnie and Mickey Mouse, 1934: $1

Lionel electric Hudson steam locomotive set, 1937: $75

Wood train, without track or power; diesel engine, three passenger cars, and one observation car, 1944: $2.39

Electric work train set with steam engine, tender, gondola, lumber car, caboose, crossing signal, crossing gate, lamppost, semaphore, 12 right-of-way signs, 12 telephone poles, and 10-foot oval track, 1954: $20

Railroad crossing sign, with flashing light, 1955: $1.87

Marx electric train set with twin-diesel engines, 3 passenger cars, and 12-foot oval track, 1955: $19.65

Happi-Time electric train set with 12-wheel steam engine, tender, boxcar, tank car, gondola, caboose and 15-foot oval track, 1956: $23.98

Lionel electric steam freight train set including smoke-belching engine with headlight, tender, tank car, flat car with cargo of pipes, boxcar and caboose; 15-piece figure-eight track, 1966: $19.88

WARTIME TOYS

With staples like tin and rubber redeployed to the war effort, the toy makers of World War II were hard-pressed to come up with the dolls and model trains, tin cars, rubber balls and bicycles that had previously carried the Christmas season.

Fortunately, as every child knows, the toy industry is endlessly creative, and no toy maker worth his wind-up key was willing to let children go toyless during those dark and doubtful days. With almost every kid's dad, uncle, big brother, or cousin already overseas or waiting for Uncle Sam's famous greetings to arrive, war interest was keen, especially—but not exclusively—among boys, so manufacturers hurried to make the most of it.

In fact, the industry had begun retooling even before America entered the war. Shortly before Pearl Harbor, at the annual Toy Manufacturer's exhibition in New York, toy-sized tanks, submarines, battleships, and aircraft appeared, all modeled after real equipment and bearing accurate markings and insignia. The next year, with America in the war, the number and variety of "militoys," as their makers called them, increased, and as the war progressed each newly designed piece of equipment—from aircraft carriers to jeeps to the famous Boeing B-17 Flying Fortress—was replicated, almost always in nonrationed materials like wood, fiberboard, and cardboard.

SANTA'S SHOPPING LIST

Wooden tank with movable turret, 1944: $2.12

Land, Sea, and Air set, including 2 jeeps, 2 planes (P-38 and P-39 models), one battle cruiser, one troop transport ship, and two freighters, all in plastic, each about 5 inches long, 1944: $1.89

Army transport plane filled with candy, 1944: $.49

Happi-Time 21-piece military airport set with cardboard buildings, paper air strip, 3 planes, detour and road-crossing signs, and bulldozer, tractor, cement mixer and dump truck for keeping things shipshape, 1945: $1.59

Pre-flight trainer: Realistic fiberboard instrument panel with throttle control, rudder pedals, and crosshairs bombsight; how-to-fly booklet, 1945: $1.89

New . . . New . . . New . . . Military-Type "Trainers"

"FLIGHT TRAINER"—FOR JR. AIRMEN!

8.95

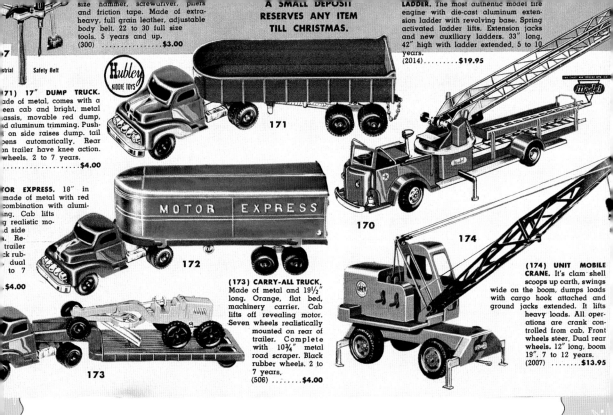

size hammer, screwdriver, pliers and friction tape. Made of extra-heavy, full grain leather, adjustable body belt. 22 to 30 full size tools. 5 years and up.
(300) $3.00

7

strial   Safety Belt

Hubley KIDDIE TOYS

71) 17" DUMP TRUCK. ade of metal, comes with a een cab and bright, metal assis, movable red dump, d aluminum trimming. Push-on side raises dump. tail ens automatically. Rear n trailer have knee action. wheels. 2 to 7 years.
...................$4.00

171

OR EXPRESS. 18" in made of metal with red combination with alumi-ng. Cab lifts g realistic mo-d side . Re-trailer ck rub-, dual to 7

$4.00

MOTOR EXPRESS

172

170

174

LADDER. The most authentic model fire engine with die-cast aluminum extension ladder with revolving base. Spring activated ladder lifts. Extension jacks and new auxiliary ladders. 33" long, 42" high with ladder extended. 5 to 10 years.
(2014)........$19.95

Model

(174) UNIT MOBILE CRANE. It's clam shell scoops up earth, swings wide on the boom, dumps loads with cargo hook attached and ground jacks extended. It lifts heavy loads. All operations are crank controlled from cab. Front wheels steer. Dual rear wheels. 12" long, boom 19". 7 to 12 years.
(2007) $13.95

173

(173) CARRY-ALL TRUCK. Made of metal and 19½" long. Orange, flat bed, machinery carrier. Cab lifts off revealing motor. Seven wheels realistically mounted on rear of trailer. Complete with 10¾" metal road scraper. Black rubber wheels. 2 to 7 years.
(506) $4.00

A WORLD ON WHEELS

It's one of America's biggest industries, with thousands of new designs each year, millions of models rolling off assembly lines, and a keen awareness of the need to keep the customer satisfied. I'm talking about the auto industry—not the one for grown-ups, the one for children. No sooner had the automobile been invented than toy cars began appearing in toy store windows at Christmas time.

Chances are, you have a distant memory from your childhood of a small, tough little vehicle, paint flaked off, wheels on their way out but still in working condition. And if you stepped on it barefoot, because it was too small to really notice, your foot sustained a lot more damage than the car. Chances are, it was made by the Dowst Company of Chicago, credited for pioneering the die-cast toy car in the 1920s. Named Tootsietoys, after a Dowst granddaughter, the small vehicles (most were no longer than three inches) were an immediate success. During the Depression, when many boys could not hope for electric trains or shiny fire engines, Tootsietoys made many Christmas morning appearances. They came in a variety of styles and models, from taxicabs to trucks to touring cars, and were so modestly priced boys could enjoy the luxury of building a collection.

1920s: Tootsietoys cars arrive on the market.

1952: Matchbox cars debut in England.

1954: Matchbox cars imported for sale in America.

1947: The first Tonka Toys are produced: the model #100 steam shovel and model #150 crane and clam.

Best of all, Tootsietoys were virtually indestructible, the sturdy bodies lasting long after their paint had flaked away and the wheels were worn to mere nibs. The company was well-established enough to survive the metal shortages of World War II and didn't meet any real competition until the 1950s, when Matchbox cars came along and became an instant stocking-stuffer favorite (see pages 109 to 110, Twenty Classic Stocking Stuffers).

While Tootsietoys was going small, another company—Tonka— decided to go tough. It all started innocently enough, when a small group of Minnesota teachers founded a business to manufacture steel garden tools and closet accessories. Along the way, they acquired a competing company that had manufactured two metal toys, a crane and clam and a steam shovel. Although neither had sold well, the teachers recognized the appeal of toys that would stand up to a lifetime's worth of play. They altered the designs to create a more realistic look, added bright paint, and reintroduced the toys in 1947. They were an immediate success, selling over 37,000 models over the next twelve months. The company quickly expanded the line, adding dump trucks, wreckers, moving vans and semis. By 1956, more than two dozen different models were available, with realistic details like chrome grilles and hubcaps, working tailgates, and hydraulics mechanisms. One fire truck came with a hose that pumped real water. But the company's signature truck didn't come along until 1965, when the Mighty Dump was introduced.

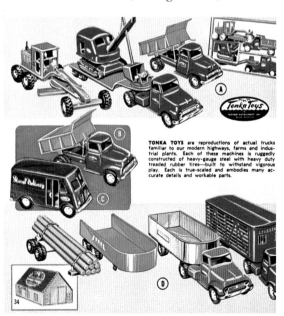

TONKA TOYS are reproductions of actual trucks familiar to our modern highways, farms and industrial plants. Each of these machines is ruggedly constructed of heavy-gauge steel with heavy duty treaded rubber tires—built to withstand vigorous play. Each is true-scaled and embodies many accurate details and workable parts.

Boys loved its bright yellow paint and its size. It soon became the company's all-time best-selling toy and, eventually, the best-selling truck in America.

In the 1960s, technology took the toy car market by storm. Until then, wheels had been largely cosmetic. But Elliot Handler, co-founder of Mattel, decided to add axles and make a gravity-powered car. With a raised back end and lowered front, the car was unbeatable on a downhill slope, and could reach the equivalent of three hundred miles an hour in a life-sized car. Watching the toy in action, Handler observed, "Wow, those are hot wheels," and the new car got its name. The Hot Wheels series, introduced in 1968, were fantasy sports cars, low-slung and racy and just what boys wanted. They sold even better than Mattel expected and became a classic American toy.

TS0644-4 "Baracuda"

TS0640-8 "T-Bird"

TS0642-6 "Silhouette"
TS0643-5 "Deora"

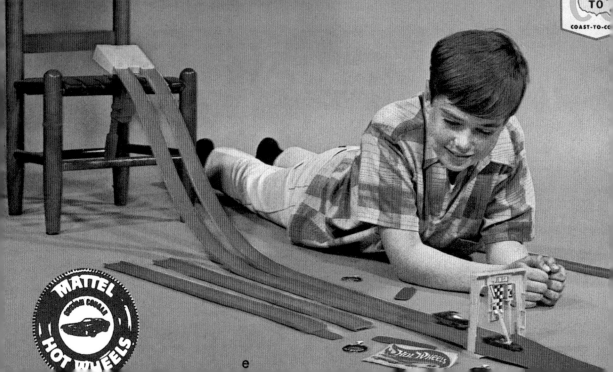

e

The other car crush of the 1960s was slot cars—electrically powered toy cars that ran on a grooved track. Actually, Lionel had introduced a slot car toy in 1912. But trains were still the big thing then, and the ability to control the car's speed was only offered as a pricey extra. The toy didn't catch on with children, and production was discontinued three years later. For the next several decades, slot-car racing was a largely adult hobby, popular with mechanically minded men who could tinker with the system to enhance and control speed. Then, in 1960, a new engine design allowed Aurora Plastics to introduce a Model Motoring set with a smaller car, more compact track, and lower price tag. The speedy little cars fascinated Americans. Countless sets appeared under Christmas trees, and extra cars could be bought separately. By 1963, Aurora had put over 1.5 million slot cars on tiny tracks across America. That year, they introduced an improved motor and used it in a new car, the Thunderjet-500 and its successor, the AFX—the best-selling slot cars in history. Although some European makers entered the market, slot cars were always more popular in America than anywhere else on earth, with a popularity boom that lasted into the 1970s and sold tens of millions of cars—enough to make Ford and GM green with envy.

SANTA'S SHOPPING LIST

Aluminum tractor set, with tractor and driver, hayrake, trailer with "dumping feature," plow, mower with moving cutter bar, and road scraper, 1949: $3.66

Coca-Cola truck, with 9 cases of Coke and a tiny hand-truck for making deliveries, 1955: $1.79

Tonka's Suburban Pumper fire truck, with fire hydrant that can be hooked to a garden hose to supply the truck's 40-inch fire hose, 1956: $8.98

Marx battery-powered bulldozer, weighs 7 pounds, can climb 50-degree grades and pull 200 pounds, 1960: $15

Truck mounted with missile launcher, "roars, then screeches as 'missile' is hurled 25 to 30 feet," 1966: $7.44

Tonka 27-inch steel car carrier with 3 plastic cars, 1966: $5.99

Aurora slot car set, 15 feet of track (5 straight, 8 curved, 1 bump, and 2 bridge sections), 2 variable speed controllers and 2 cars (2 ½ inches long, 600mph scale speed), 1966: $13.88

GTO Torture Track by Motorific, with car and 61-piece multilevel track, 1966: $11.99

Extra cars for Motorific track, choice of Corvette Stingray, Ford T-Bird, Pontiac Grand Prix, or Jaguar XKE, 1966: $1.99 each

MODEL KITS

Of course, if you didn't like the toy planes and cars in the store, you could always ask Santa to bring you one you could make yourself.

Do-it-yourself models had been around since early in the twentieth century. Made of thin balsa wood, they were fine for what they were but could never hope to have the intricate detail of the real thing. Then, in the years before and during the war, enormous strides were made in the plastic industry. The future really was plastic, and for the first time it became possible to mold the strong but intricately detailed pieces needed for models. At the same time, the nation's war experience made millions of boys vehicle aficionados. From jeeps to battleships to Japanese Zeros, the average American boy carried a catalog of war machines in his head, and his fingers itched to play with the real thing. With metal shortages in effect, toy manufacturers offered boys a chance to make their own toys from wood or plastic, positioning kits as a new and exciting way to get the exact replica they wanted.

Popular model makers during the war were Cleveland and Joe Ott. Revell introduced its first all-plastic kit in 1951. The model in question wasn't a war vehicle but a classic car, a 1910 Maxwell. It was so successful that the company brought out a whole line of classic car kits. Over the next decade, as automobiles became better designed, more colorful,

and a symbol of American speed and luxury, cars became a staple. In fact, there was almost nothing that couldn't be had in model version, and almost every boy's bedroom proudly displayed a model of something—be it a Mercury capsule, a low-slung race car, or a jazzy aircraft carrier.

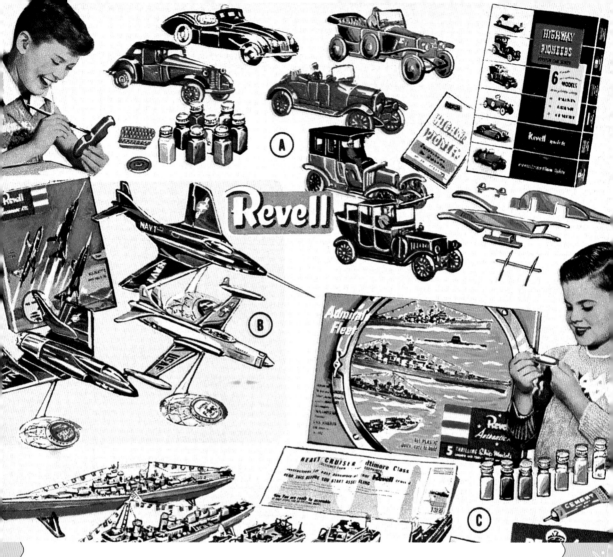

SANTA'S SHOPPING LIST

Lockheed Lightning P38 or German Messerschmitt ME, 36-inch wingspan, 1944: $1.33

20-inch Navy destroyer, wood parts, paint not included: $.87

Deluxe "real-wing" construction RAF Spitfire or Japanese Zero (Mitsubishi OO) airplanes, approximately 30-inch wingspan, 1944: $2.69

11 ½-inch Army jeep, wood and fiberboard parts: composite wheels, decals, and olive drab paint included, 1944: $2.27

50-part MG-style sportscar, 15 inches long, 1954: $10.95

Revell set of 3 jet fighters with display stands, includes the Lockheed Starfire, Gruman Cougar, and Chance Vought Cutlass, each with 18-inch wingspan, 1955: $1.98

Gilbert Skyflash model plane, flies on real gasoline engine, 1962: $19.98

CARROM

A

B

OFFICIAL RULES for the Tudor TRU-ACTION

D

CHECKER GAME

NORTHWESTERN PRODUCTS

I'd Like to Buy a Hotel:

GAMES FROM MONOPOLY TO TWISTER

The muted tumble of dice, the *knock-knock-knock* of markers counting off spaces, the anticipation of summoning Miss Scarlet to the Conservatory with the lead pipe, and the happy realization that, because it was Christmas, you could probably coax mom or dad into playing along with you . . . No wonder games were one of the most popular gifts of the mid-twentieth century.

THE GOLDEN AGE OF BOARD GAMES

For thousands of years, board games were largely abstract simulations of conquest and strategy, and they were played mostly by men. Board games that appealed to women and children didn't come along until the second half of the nineteenth century. Most of these games, such as Mansion of Happiness,

How do you bring the game of "Pin the Tail on the Donkey" up to date — or shouldn't I ask.

Harriet Nelson to her son Ricky, *The Adventures of Ozzie and Harriet*, 1952

Snakes and Ladders, and the Checkered Game of Life were intended to help children learn to make moral choices that would lead to a happy life. However, children weren't the only ones who played—The Checkered Game of Life was a national sensation. It sold over 45,000 copies in 1861 and was reproduced in a travel size so Civil War soldiers could carry it with them.

Another early game based on moral values was called the Landlord's Game. Created by

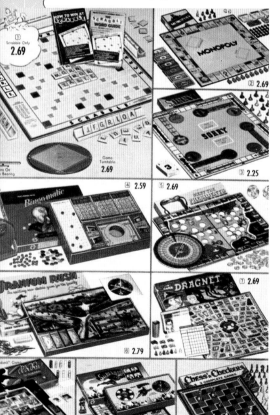

Elizabeth Magie in the early years of the twentieth century, the game was supposed to demonstrate the ills caused by unequal distribution of wealth. To Magie's chagrin, it did nothing of the sort. Instead of learning compassion for the poor, players schemed to accumulate larger piles of wealth. Even worse, they positively loved seeing their fellow-players swept into bankruptcy. Unwilling to reconfigure her game to appeal to the ignoble side of human nature, Magie could not interest a major manufacturer in it, and the Landlord's Game was left to languish. It would resurface with a new name three decades later to become the most successful board game of the century.

THE 1930s

One of the most popular children's board games of the 1930s was a strategy game invented at the tail end of the Roaring '20s. Called Hop Ching

Checkers, the game featured a board with a colorful six-pointed star, neatly pocketed to hold players' marbles as they plotted to move them from one star point to the opposite point. Aside from being colorful and new, the game was also exotic. The name conjured the distant and ancient: fire-breathing dragons decorated the corners of the board. Hop Ching Checkers was a craze throughout the 1930s and remained popular for several decades, though it's better known today simply as Chinese checkers. The game, by the way, was neither Asian nor ancient—

SPELL IT—delights youngsters ages 4 to 10 years

Amazing game with the magic doors! Spells, adds, multiplies, subtracts. Operates just like a telephone dial. Children dial letters to spell objects pictured on board. Open the magic door—if word is spelled correctly a picture of the object appears. When arithmetic problem are dialed correctly, answer is shown. Educational fun for 1 or more. Heavy cardboard 17 inches square.
49 N 207—Shipping weight 1 pound 4 ounces. $1.79

$1.12 Treasure Hunt. Party vorite. Scramble for ure Hunt cards; win pirate mone For 2-16 players—all ages. Cou letters, money in 8¼x5½-in. che 49 N 170—Shipping weight 1 pound 6 ounces . . . . $1.

Original Games by Cadaco-Ellis

"father having been a little boy, suspicions me when jest 'fore Christmas I'm good as I kin be."

the name was chosen to lend a foreign touch and play on the 1920s' infatuation with the Chinese and Japanese cultures.

In spite of—or perhaps because of—the hard times of the Depression, wealth and property games were a hallmark of the 1930s. First came Finance, a revised version of Elizabeth Magie's Landlord's Game, with new rules that made wealth accumulation the goal of the game. A few years after Finance hit the market, another version of the Landlord's Game, Parker Brothers' Monopoly, was the talk of the 1935 Toy Fair. With houses and hotels, a regular allowance of two hundred dollars every time you passed Go, and brightly colored properties based on street names in Atlantic City, Monopoly was a frolicsome oasis in the midst of the Depression. It sold more than twenty thousand sets in its first week on the market and by Christmas was the best-selling game in America.

Fittingly, there were real legal entanglements, lawyers, and big money at stake. The creators of Finance claimed that Monopoly's rules were almost identical to its own.

Monopoly's creators felt the same way about Milton Bradley's Easy Money, which appeared the next year. In the end, Parker Brothers used some of Monopoly's earnings to buy rights to both games.

In recent years, special-edition Monopoly sets have been created for every city, locale, interest, and event imaginable. But this isn't really a new marketing strategy. Buckopoly, a set created for Ohio Buckeye fans, appeared as early as 1947. As for the plump, banker-ish little gentleman who serves as the game's mascot, he wasn't part of the original design at all. Rumored to be modeled on a Parker Brothers salesman, with a dash of J. P. Morgan thrown in, he didn't make his appearance until the 1936, when he appeared on both Monopoly and Finance boxes, and he didn't receive a name until 1946, when he appeared on Parker Brothers' Rich Uncle game and was dubbed Rich Uncle Pennybags.

During the Depression, board games were an inexpensive form of family entertainment. Games from previous decades that had been played on expensive boards, such as chess, Parcheesi, and backgammon, were issued in cardboard editions, and new board games flourished. Sorry! (a simplified version of Parcheesi that had come out a year ahead of Monopoly) sold well for the next several decades, without once cutting into the Parcheesi market. The first radio quiz show, *Professor Quiz*, aired on CBS in 1936 and was quickly followed by *Information Please* and several others. Their emphasis on knowledge gave new popularity to games like Go to the Head of the Class, the Electric Questioner, Anagrams, and Criss Cross Words (an early version of Scrabble).

WARTIME GAMES

Board games might have remained a fad of the '30s had the war not come along. Toys that would ordinarily top Christmas wish lists—bicycles, rubber dolls, tin soldiers, and electric train sets—were generally unavailable, either because they required materials in short supply or because their manufacturers were busy with war work. Games, however, were produced in record numbers. Paper and cardboard were still available, and the government encouraged people to enjoy games as a way of keeping up morale on the home front. New games reflected the nation's war interests and had names like Democracy, Tactics, Flagship, and Our Defenders. Old games were refitted for the new war years. A card game called Victory Rummy appeared less than a year after Pearl Harbor, while Bingo was reborn as Victo, with red, white, and blue cards and pieces. Ironically, the enduring game of the war years had nothing to do with war, nor was it new. Chutes and Ladders, a game for children who had not yet learned to read, was the old game of Snakes and Ladders with the moral teachings removed. It was simple to understand, required no reading, and was an instant hit.

BOOMER BOARDS

You can probably picture it now . . . the Peppermint Stick Forest, the Gumdrop Mountain, and the iceberg-like Ice Cream Floats . . . not to mention the ultimate goal, the Candy Castle. Since its debut in 1949, more children remember Candy Land as their first board game than any other.

It was all part of the new, child-friendly postwar world. Realizing that there was a huge new population of young gamesters out there, manufacturers went to work. Soon a cornucopia of games specifically designed for children was pouring forth. Many, like Candy Land, were new and original. Others were adult games retrofitted for the youth market, such as Scrabble for Juniors and Bridge for Juniors. In a mid-'50s game called Junior Executive, players ran businesses like toy stores, soda fountains, and ice cream shops.

Television had an enormous impact on boomer era games. Dozens of children's shows, airing daily after school and dominating Saturday and Sunday mornings, offered a direct route to the little consumer. In addition to being ideal advertising venues, these shows created opportunities for hundreds of new games. From *Rin-Tin-*

SANTA'S SHOPPING LIST
Monopoly, 1944: popular edition, $1.79; deluxe set, $2.88

Sorry!, 1944: $1.32

TOP-ography, 1944: $1.83

Finance, 1947: $1.32

Uncle Wiggly, 1947: $.67

Chinese checkers, with marbles, 1949: $1.10

Parcheesi, 1949: $.92

Candy Land, 1954: $2

Go to the Head of the Class, 1955: $2.50

Chutes and Ladders, 1955: $2

Scrabble, 1966: $3.17

Scrabble for Juniors, 1966: $2.44

Tin to *Gilligan's Island*, *Huckleberry Hound* to *Bewitched*, there was hardly a show that didn't have a game of its own. No sooner had Disneyland opened in 1955 than board games based on its enticing environments—such as Tomorrowland, Fantasyland, Frontierland, and Adventure-land—appeared.

In addition to television tie-ins, there were games based on popular children's movies, such as *The Sword in the Stone* and *Mary Poppins*. Movie tie-ins weren't new— there had been Shirley Temple games in the '30s, and *The Game of the Wizard of Oz*

in 1939. The difference in the 1950s and '60s was the vast expansion of the child-oriented universe. Even fictional characters like Nancy Drew, the Hardy Boys, and Barbie had their own board games.

For the most part the charm of these games lay in the glow of the tie-in. A few classic games did come out of the era, though. For its hundredth anniversary, the Milton Bradley Company decided to re-vamp its original hit, the Checkered Game of Life. Designers replaced the checker-board grid of the original game with a track on which car-shaped playing pieces col-lected rewards like paychecks and job pro-motions while trying to save for retirement, resist loans at twenty-five-percent interest, and avoid bankruptcy brought on by spend-ing and taxes. It was a great set-up for adult life, and the game became an instant hit.

Perhaps the most popular game of the era was Risk, from Parker Brothers. Designed by French film director Albert Lamorisse (*The Red Balloon*), it had been released as La Conquête du Monde in France in 1957. For its 1959 U.S. version, it was renamed and slightly modified. Although the game could not duplicate all conditions of war—uncer-tain weather, battle fatigue, and the difficulty of sustaining extended campaigns—it was nevertheless considered one of the first realistic war games to appeal to a mainstream au-dience. The number of pieces involved (each player had his own army, consisting of in-fantry, cavalry, and artillery) made the game especially intriguing to boys, and Risk was considered the thinking man's game of the middle-school set.

GAME TRENDS

1920s: Hop-Ching Checkers, Mah Jongg, Uncle Wiggily

1930: Anagrams, Cavalcade

1932: Finance

1934: Sorry!

1935: Monopoly, Take Off

1936: 4-5-6 Pick Up Sticks, Big Business, Easy Money, Go to the Head of the Class

1937: Bargain Day, Jury Box, Reward!

1938: Cabby, Criss Cross Words, The Great Charlie Chan Detective Mystery Game, Tripoley

1939: Contack, The Game of the Wizard of Oz

1940: Adventures of Superman, Democracy, Dig-it, Flagship, Pocket Football, Tactics: The Game of World Strategy

1941: Ethan Allen's All-Star Baseball Game, Jingle Quiz, Quiz Kids Radio Question Bee, Top-ography

1942: Empires, Victo

1943: Chutes and Ladders, Ration Board

1944: Our Defenders

1946: Rich Uncle: Stock Market Game

1947: Buckaroo: The Cowboy Roundup Game, Game of States and Cities

1948: Scrabble

1949: Candy Land, Captain Gallant Adventure Game, Clue, Electric Football, Cooties, Roy Rogers Rodeo Game

1950: Cinderella, Hopalong Cassidy Game, Little Bo Peep, Park and Shop

1961: Barbie Queen of the Prom, Double Your Money, Face the Facts, Stratego, Twixt

1962: Acquire, By the Numbers, College Bowl, Password, Phlounder

1963: Ad-Lib Crossword Cubes, The Beverly Hillbillies Game, The Candid Camera Game, Mouse Trap

1964: Alumni Fun, Battle Line, Jeopardy, Quinto, Stocks & Bonds

1965: Blitzkrieg, Glib, Mr. President, Operation, Pirates of the Caribbean

1966: Twister

1967: The Dating Game, Facts in Five, Ker Plunk, Pounce

1952: ScareCrow

1953: Assembly Line, Keyword

1954: Beat the Clock, Down You Go

1955: Davy Crockett Indian Scouting Game, Dollar a Second, Groucho's You Bet Your Life, Junior Executive, Revlon's $64,000 Dollar Question Quiz Game, Walt Disney's Official Frontierland Game

1956: Perquackey, Yahtzee, You'll Never Get Rich

1957: Name That Tune, The Nancy Drew Mystery Game, The Wonderful Wizard of Oz

1958: The Big Board, The Gray Ghost, The Price Is Right, Scrabble for Juniors

1959: Cat & Mouse, Concentration, Risk

1960: Bozo the Clown Circus Game, Bridge for Juniors, Dave Garroway's Today Game, Dough Re Mi, Game of the States, The Game of Life Video Village

Lively games for the fam

TWISTER, the game that ties you up in knots—as funny to watch as it is to play!

[1] TWISTER. A stacking-foot game played on a vinyl game rug. Each spin requires one player to move a hand or foot into a different-colored circle on the game rug. First one to lose his balance and topple is the loser. Vinyl rug is foldable, rollable, washable, sturdy enough for countless Twister games. For two to four players and unlimited watchers. All ages. X 924-9772 A—Wt. 2 lbs. 10 oz. . 2.88

S-S-H-H-H-H: Don't wake the he'll YELL

[2] BABY SITTER GAI moves around the te sweeping the telephone, tidying up toys, and trying baby! The winner is the p the most money "doing o plastic house section wit money coins, bank cards. Ages 7 to 14. X 924-9780 A—Shpg. wt

BEYOND BOARD GAMES

Of course, board games weren't the only games to be had. Card games from the early decades of the century enjoyed a long run of popularity. Like board games, they were especially popular in the 1930s and '40s, when money and materials were scarce. Even when the shortages were over, games like Rook, Pit, Touring, and Flinch continued to find favor well into the 1960s. The most popular of these were Rook, which became the world's best-selling card game, and Pit, a commodities trading game adapted from an earlier game designed by Edgar Cayce (yes, *that* Edgar Cayce).

Many other games were spin-offs of parlor games from the past. A 1930s game called Jury Box presented a fictional murder case, complete with clues and pictures of the crime scene, and players took the roles of jury members. Games based on radio and televisions shows like The $64,000 Question and Password appeared in fresh variations almost annually. In Dig and Treasure Hunt, players fished lettered cards out of a pool, then scrambled to be the first to make a word. Other games, such as Dig-it, Ad-Lib, and Crossword Cubes, challenged players to make sentences of random phrases, usually with hilarious results.

And of course, there was Yahtzee. Invented by a Canadian couple whose only goal was to pass the time aboard their boat, the "yacht game" became one of the most popular non-board games of its time.

One of the enduring smash hit games involved an odd-looking, wholly fictional beast called the Cootie, whose body was assembled piece by piece with rolls of the dice. Cooties' inventor, a Minnesota postman named Herb Schaper, created the first sets out of wood and offered them to Dayton's, a local department

Games of Skill
for back yard or rumpus
Improve your score...
more fun every game!

store. The game was a hit, selling over a million sets in its first three years on the market, and a million sets a year thereafter. No one can quite explain why they love the odd little insect-like creature with brightly colored body parts, a curled proboscis, and a slightly quizzical expression, but the cry "I got Cooties!" has been heard amidst the ribbons and wrappings of many a Christmas.

Not all games were sedate, however. With the coming of suburbia, the American

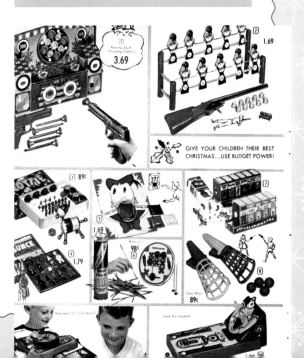

GIVE YOUR CHILDREN THEIR BEST
CHRISTMAS...USE BUDGET POWER!

home was reconfigured. Rooms were open and far less formal, configured for a lifestyle that anticipated and enjoyed a new commodity called leisure time. The must-have room was no longer a parlor but a large, open space known as a rec room or rumpus room. Often in the basement or above the garage, the rec room was a play space for children and adults alike, furnished with durable furniture and devoid of breakables. Naturally, the kids had a ball. And once manufacturers caught on, they created a whole new category of toys, such as pint-sized pool tables, bowling sets with plastic pins and ball, and golf sets with obstacles and holes that simulated an eighteen-hole course. There were target practice games with targets that spun victoriously when popped with a cork gun, pinball games, archery sets with suction-tipped arrows, and basketball hoops and balls designed for indoor play.

The rec room became a mini amusement park, and toy makers no longer had to worry about games that were loud or messy, that inspired too much shrieking or scattering of parts and pieces. A game called Bash! came with a plastic hammer and challenged players to knock pieces from a tower without toppling it. The ever-popular Operation sounded a loud buzzer at every wrong move. Did I mention that many rec rooms were ultimately fitted with soundproofing?

Then, just as the baby boomers were growing up and having their first boy-girl parties, along came one of the greatest rec room games of all time—Twister, the game that practically mandates getting closer to the opposite sex. Played on a mat of multicolored dots, with players contorting themselves into unlikely positions, it was a great ice-breaker. When Johnny Carson demonstrated it on the Tonight Show, deliciously entangling himself with Eva Gabor, America realized the game's potential and raced out to buy it. The world soon followed suit.

Though few people realized it, a great change in games was already on the horizon. In fact, the first of the new wave had already arrived. In 1949, an innocuously innovative, even gimmicky, game called Electric Football appeared in Christmas catalogs. Earlier games had claimed to be electric, but the sparks were usually confined to a battery-operated light that glowed when a correct answer was given. Electric Football was different. It featured a field that vibrated when the switch was thrown, moving the tiny men between the goals. Novelty made the game a success, and over the next years it was refined to give players more control over their team's movements. Electronic games had made their debut, opening the door to the next big thing, video and computer games.

Just Like Mom and Dad

Fads come and fads go, but there's one thing kids always want: to be a grown-up. Not even Santa could speed up the hands of time, but his toy-making elves took on the problem and delivered the next best thing—tons and tons and tons of toys scaled down to create the illusion that yes, indeed, you could fly a plane, own a house, or run a store at the tender age of eight.

FUTURE HOMEMAKERS UNITE

Children have always mimicked their parents, and twentieth-century youngsters certainly weren't the first to have small housekeeping utensils made for them. But the twentieth century saw an explosion of these small training-for-the-future toys. And many of them worked just like the real thing. As early as 1938, train maker Lionel made an all-electric range

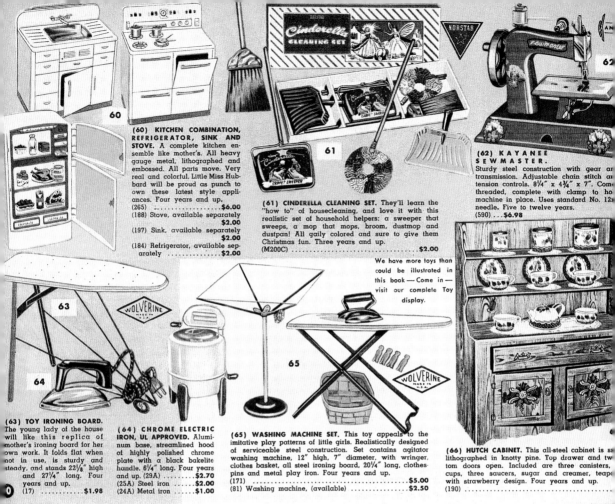

(60) KITCHEN COMBINATION, REFRIGERATOR, SINK AND STOVE. A complete kitchen ensemble like mother's. All heavy gauge metal, lithographed and embossed. All parts move. Very real and colorful. Little Miss Hubbard will be proud as punch to own these latest style appliances. Four years and up.
(265) $6.00
(188) Stove, available separately $2.00
(197) Sink, available separately $2.00
(184) Refrigerator, available separately $2.00

(61) CINDERELLA CLEANING SET. They'll learn the "how to" of housecleaning, and love it with this realistic set of household helpers: a sweeper that sweeps, a mop that mops, broom, dustmop and dustpan! All gaily colored and sure to give them Christmas fun. Three years and up.
(M200C) $2.00

(62) KAYANEE SEWMASTER. Sturdy steel construction with gear an transmission. Adjustable chain stitch an tension controls. 8¼" x 4¾" x 7". Com threaded, complete with clamp to ho machine in place. Uses standard No. 12 needle. Five to twelve years.
(590) ... $6.98

We have more toys than could be illustrated in this book — Come in — visit our complete Toy display.

(63) TOY IRONING BOARD. The young lady of the house will like this replica of mother's ironing board for her own work. It folds flat when not in use, is sturdy and steady, and stands 22⅛" high and 27¼" long. Four years and up.
(17) $1.98

(64) CHROME ELECTRIC IRON, UL APPROVED. Aluminum base, streamlined hood of highly polished chrome plate with a black bakelite handle. 6¼" long. Four years and up. (29A) $2.70
(25A) Steel iron $2.00
(24A) Metal iron $1.00

(65) WASHING MACHINE SET. This toy appeals to the imitative play patterns of little girls. Realistically designed of serviceable steel construction. Set contains agitator washing machine, 12" high, 7" diameter, with wringer, clothes basket, all steel ironing board, 20¼" long, clothespins and metal play iron. Four years and up.
(171) $5.00
(81) Washing machine, (available) $2.50

(66) HUTCH CABINET. This all-steel cabinet is s lithographed in knotty pine. Top drawer and tw tom doors open. Included are three canisters, cups, three saucers, sugar and creamer, teapo with strawberry design. Four years and up.
(190) ....

for little girls, beating the Easy-Bake Oven by twenty-five years. The growing number of electrical appliances available made their toy versions more intriguing to children, and for the first time in history housekeeping toys weren't just for little girls. The little boy who would never have wanted a pint-sized washtub could be seen happily pushing a toy vacuum cleaner around the house or asking for a mini malt machine of his own. Thus, the arrival of mass-produced, less-expensive toys and a rising middle class that allowed children more play time helped fuel the boom in homemaking toys, and the postwar focus on suburban domesticity really got things rolling. The number of items, as well as their detail and authenticity, was truly breathtaking. Many young girls would not be so well-equipped for homemaking until their bridal showers and wedding gifts arrived years later.

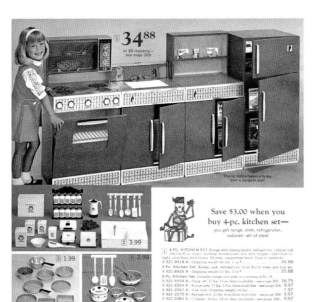

EASY-BAKE OVEN

Most of the thousands of mini gadgets and appliances made for kids were generic—except for one, a name that has appeared on thousands of wish-lists since the moment it arrived—the Easy-Bake Oven. Introduced by Kenner in 1964, most people regarded it as America's first working toy oven. That wasn't true—working electric toy ovens had been produced since the 1930s. No one especially cared, though. With its au-courant designer colors and ingenious lightbulb baking system, the Easy-Bake Oven was a definite first of some kind. It was a Christmas best-seller, and by the end of its first year on the market over half a million aspiring bakers were proud owners. The little oven's appeal to children proved timeless, weathering the antidomestic flavor of the 1970s and the onslaught of techno-toys after that. By the end of the twentieth century, over sixteen million Easy-Bake Ovens had been sold, and it remains available. Whoever knew you could have so much fun with a lightbulb?

SANTA'S SHOPPING LIST

Washday set with washtub, washboard, stand-alone drying rack, folding ironing board, iron, and clothespins, 1944: $.94; deluxe set includes washtub stand, laundry basket, and extra clothespins: $1.88

Plastic tea service for 4 in fiesta colors, with red plastic cups and cake plates, blue saucers, green pitcher with red lid and ivory base, ivory cream pitcher, ivory sugar bowl with red lid, and paper napkins adorned with Scottie dog and plaid border, 1944: $1.59

Glasbake tot-sized glass oven set "just like Mom's," with 4 baking dishes, loaf pan, covered casserole, oval baking dish, and deep dish pie plate, 1945: $1.24

Glass lemonade set with pitcher, 4 tumblers, and wooden glass caddy, 1945: $.89

Housecleaning set with carpet sweeper that boasts "thorough brush action and dust pick up just like Mother's," apron, broom, dust mop, and dust pan, 1947: $2.79

Electric stove with working oven and burners, white enamel, 15 inches tall, 1947: $7.39

Electric iron, 6 ¼ inches long, 1947: $1.69

Little Baker Mixer Maker with stand, bowl, and crank handle that "whips real cream," 1947: $1.69

Polished aluminum cook set with muffin tin, mixing bowl, cake pan, frying pan, pie plate, Jell-O mold, 2 fancy cake molds, 4 cookie cutters, cookie sheet, roasting pan with lid, measuring cup, scoop, and spoons, 1950: $1.19

Washday set with white enameled agitator-type machine with wringer, stand-alone drying rack, folding ironing board, iron, laundry basket, and clothespins, 1950: $3.59

Kid-E-Kitchen fold-open cabinet with dishpan, dishrack, mat, sink strainer, apron, dish services and silverware for 2, includes sponge, dish mop, dishcloth, bottle brush, dish towel, and real Ajax, Vel, and Brillo pads, 1954: $2.98

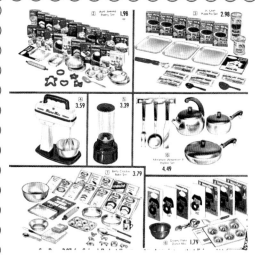

Cake Box Set includes metal canister set, cake box, and bread box, all in metal with blue Delft design, along with spoon, cookie cutters, and rolling pin, 1954: $1

Fully equipped cardboard broom closet with upper shelf and carpet sweeper, broom, dust mop, sponge mop, dust pan, hand duster, dust cloth, Brillo pads, Palmolive soap, dusting mitt, and apron, 1955: $2.98

Vacuum cleaner that "actually picks up dust, ashes, and paper" with light-up head and removable dust bag, batteries required, 1955: $3.98

Battery-powered Micro-Mix stand mixer with bowl and beater, 1955: $3.59

Betty Crocker Junior Baking Kit with cookie, cake, and frosting mixes, as well as mixing bowl, utensils, baking pans, cookie sheet, cookie cutters, muffin tin, and recipe book, 1955: $3.79

Original Kenner Easy-Bake Oven, in avocado green, 1963: $15.99

Electric vacuum, front light, with 12-foot cord, 1966: $9.44

Suzy Homemaker washing machine, just add soap and water and set for wash, jet wash, or spin dry, 1966: $9.99

133-piece bake set includes mixing bowl and spoons, 4 pudding bowls and spoons, rolling pin, muffin tin, measuring spoons, cake decorator with 3 nozzles, 2 gingerbread man cutters, 9 cookie cutters, cookie sheet, 2 round cake pans, 2 loaf cake pans, 2 pie pans, 2 sheets of fortune cookie sayings, 36 birthday candles and recipe book; boxed mixes include 12 cakes, 10 frosting, 3 decorator, 8 cookie, 9 pudding, 2 pie crust, 2 apple filling, 3 gingerbread, 2 brownie, 2 cream puff, 2 biscuit, 1966: $8.99

Electric Magic-Cool oven with see-through double glass door, with mixing bowl, cake pan, pie pan, muffin cups, mixing bowl, spoon, measuring spoon, rolling pin, recipe book and 6 mixes, 1966: $8.44

Early-America style spice rack with 10 plastic jars and lids, 1966: $1.49

40-piece plastic fruit and vegetable set, 1967: $1.19

BABIES ON BOARD

Until the coming of the fashion doll in the mid-1950s, most dolls were infants and children, meant to be cuddled and cared for by the little girl who was their mommy. She played at dressing and feeding them, at washing their clothes and tucking them in at night. But in the baby-centered post-war years, being a doll mother, just like being a real mother, became a much more elaborate undertaking. Newfangled items like diaper bags, bottle sterilizers, and playpens came on the market. Dolly, it seemed, had to have them all. Never had so many elaborate little accessories been created for someone who was, after all, only a toy herself.

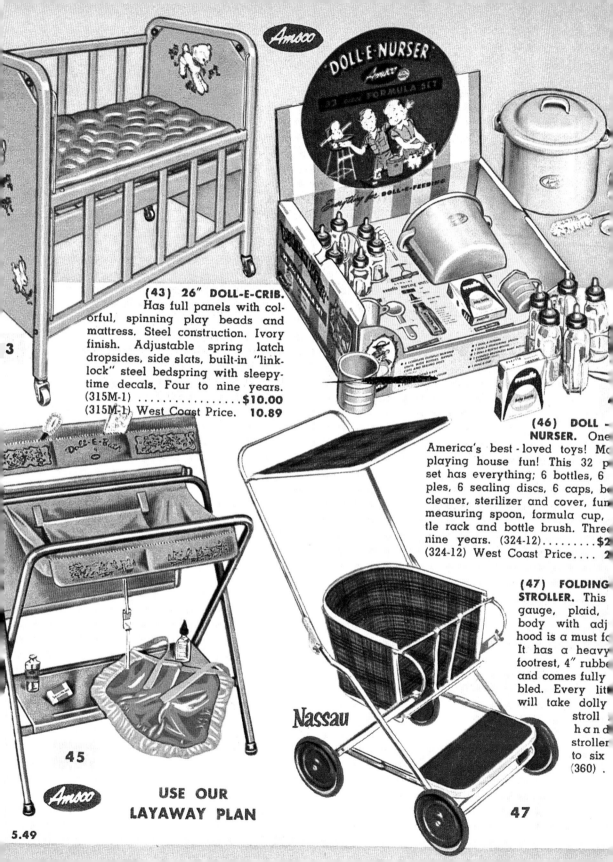

Amsco

'DOLL-E-NURSER'
Amsco
32 PIECE FORMULA SET

Everything for DOLL-E-FEEDING

(43) 26" DOLL-E-CRIB.
Has full panels with colorful, spinning play beads and mattress. Steel construction. Ivory finish. Adjustable spring latch dropsides, side slats, built-in "link-lock" steel bedspring with sleepy-time decals. Four to nine years.
(315M-1) $10.00
(315M-1) West Coast Price. 10.89

(46) DOLL -
NURSER. One
America's best - loved toys! Mo
playing house fun! This 32 p
set has everything; 6 bottles, 6
ples, 6 sealing discs, 6 caps, be
cleaner, sterilizer and cover, fun
measuring spoon, formula cup,
tle rack and bottle brush. Three
nine years. (324-12)........$2
(324-12) West Coast Price.... 2

(47) FOLDING
STROLLER. This
gauge, plaid,
body with adj
hood is a must fo
It has a heavy
footrest, 4" rubbe
and comes fully
bled. Every lit
will take dolly
stroll
h a n d
stroller
to six
(360) .

Nassau

45

Amsco

**USE OUR
LAYAWAY PLAN**

47

5.49

3

ALL ABOUT THE HOUSE

Once upon a time, playing house meant setting up a few pieces of cast-off furniture. With the coming of mass production and an affluent middle class, toy makers broadened their focus to make furniture that was a tot-sized replica of the real thing. Add to this toy replicas of almost everything Mom and Dad had, and you could create your own little midcentury modern dream house—without the mortgage.

SANTA'S SHOPPING LIST

Toy telephone in "genuine ivory plastic," 1944: $1.89

Hardwood table and 2 chairs, painted ivory with blue, red and green Pennsylvania Dutch decorations, red finials on the table and chairs, red seats, 1944: $19.95

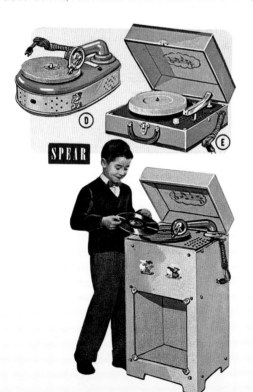

Red wooden rocking chair with cushioned seat upholstered in red-and-black plaid, 1945: $3.98

Steel kitchen cabinet, stocked with packages of play food, 1947: $1.49

Woven rattan rocking chair, painted ivory with green trim and floral seat cushion, 1949: $5.49

GE console model record player, with storage shelf for LPs, 1949: $36.95

Fiberboard fireplace with glowing electric logs, 1950: $2.49

Picnic table and benches, finished hardwood, 1950: $12.95

Drop-leaf, maple-finish pine table and two chairs, 1950: $5.89

China hutch, steel with lithographed knotty pine pattern, comes with canister set, cups and saucers, teapot, sugar bowl, and creamer, 1954: $4

TV/hostess trays, use trays alone or with folding stand, set of two, 1955: $1.49

Swivel platform overstuffed rocker, 1955: $11.95

Yellow Formica kitchen table and 2 chairs with chrome legs and plastic padded seats and backs, 1955: $14.95

Same features found in Dad's chair . . . Jr. TV viewers can safely rock or swivel around in perfect comfort.

— Spiegel Christmas catalog, 1955

Copper-tone kitchen appliances suite with nonworking stove and refrigerator, working double sink, cupboard, and play food packages, appliances are steel with coppertone-finish, 1966: $34.88

Plastic china buffet in French provincial style, ivory with gold trim, 2 drawers and 3 cupboards, 58-piece tea service and accessories included, 1966: $13.47

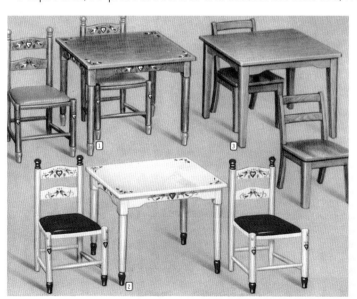

Kenner Change-A-Channel TV set with cartridges of 12 popular shows, 1966: $12.88; additional show cartridges, $1.88 each

Early American–style vinyl-upholstered loveseat with vinyl upholstery, 1966: $15.44; matching rocking chair, $9.44

Ultra-modern "Swedish-style" dinette set with pedestal legs and 2 swivel chairs, 1966: $29.95

I'm grown up!

— June Allyson, *My Man Godfrey*, 1957

CAREER DAY

Children of all societies have had scaled-down toys that helped them hone the skills they would need for adult life, but toys that let children playfully explore the world of work are a distinctly twentieth-century idea, products of a society where children have the leisure to try on adult occupations and the luxury of choice.

Even the most famous "career" toy—the doctor bag, introduced by the Pressman Toy Corporation in 1922—wasn't meant for would-be doctors but for frightened young patients, to help them overcome their jitters. It was children themselves who took the little bag seriously, and soon other toys were helping children dream big. The much-criticized fashion doll trend of the mid-1950s was, for some girls, a way of exploring clothing construction and design, while boys who built with Lincoln Logs quickly learned the meaning of "load-bearing wall." It wasn't long until toy makers began mining more esoteric professions. Visions of sugar plums may have danced in the heads of nineteenth-century children, but for twentieth-century children it was more likely to be visions of toys that let them be store owners, movie makers, junior accountants, dress designers, and a hundred other things.

SANTA'S SHOPPING LIST

Mannequin doll for the future fashion designer, comes with dress form, patterns, and fabric for 4 outfits, 1944: $3.59

Complete photographer's kit includes Trailblazer camera and everything needed to take and develop pictures, 1949: $5.75

Red cash register, play money included, 1950: $2.79

Deluxe children's typewriter, "not just another toy," 1950: $13.95

36-piece carpenter's set in steel box inlcudes T-square, adjustable plane, ruler, carpenter's pencil, hand drill with 9 drill bits, pliers, wrench, crow bar, claw hammer, wood chisels and more, 1951: $8.90

Dennis the Menace Dentist Set, with silver instruments for examining, filling, extracting, and cleaning, along with play dentures and a conveniently mute patient, 1954: $5.00

Dollies and pets make excellent patients.

— Sears Christmas catalog, 1944

Cub Printing Press with ink, rubber type, hand-crank press, and paper — "it can be the beginning of a lifetime career in journalism or printing," 1954: $3.98

Mechanical drawing set for the budding draftsman or engineer, includes drawing board, T-square, ruler, protractor, triangles, pencils, pens, paper, ink, and manuals, 1954: $4.95

Super market checkout counter, lithographed steel equipped with working cash register, divider to separate customers groceries and pull items forward. grocery cart, two dozen play packages of food, and paper grocery bags, 1955: $5.69

Penneys Deluxe Typewriter
* Types all the characters you need—even upper and lower case letters
* Includes margin ruler and other features of the bigger machines

15.99

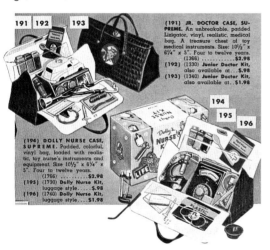

(191) JR. DOCTOR CASE, SU-PREME. An unbreakable, padded Lizigator, vinyl, realistic, medical bag. A treasure chest of toy medical instruments. Size: 10½" x 6¼" x 5". Four to twelve years.
(1366) $2.98
(192) (1330) Junior Doctor Kit, also available at...$.98
(193) (1340) Junior Doctor Kit, also available at...$1.98

(194) DOLLY NURSE CASE, SUPREME. Padded, colorful, vinyl bag, loaded with realistic, toy nurse's instruments and equipment. Size 10½" x 6¼" x 5". Four to twelve years.
(1766) $2.98
(195) (1730) Dolly Nurse Kit, luggage style . . . $.98
(196) (1740) Dolly Nurse Kit, luggage style . . . $1.98

Doll hospital with "fever" doll that flushes, hospital bed, rubber gloves, thermometer, and 13 other instruments, and doctor's bag should a house call be needed, 1955: $3.98

Adding machine "for junior bookkeepers," totals up to 9,999, 1955: $1.79

Switchboard "has everything a little 'operator' could want," including plug-in cords, plug in holes with red and green lights, levers to make bells ring, dial and receiver on switchboard, and 2 desk phones with cords, 1955: $5.95

Suzy-Q Secret Agent set, with garter holster, necklace I.D. badge, decoder glasses, shoulder strap bag containing lipstick pistol, radio compact, and secret writing pencil, 1966: $3.49

Cardboard grocery store counter with cash register, telephone for taking orders, display shelves, and packages of play food, 1966: $4.77

James Bond 007 Attache Case, equipped with secret compartment, 4-piece sniper's rifle, automatic pistol, Luger-type pistol, code-O-matic, code book, booby trap, and passport, 1967: $10.99

JUST LIKE GRANDAD: COWBOY MANIA

Imagine an entire nation of gun-slingers and cowgirls, brave sheriffs, daring outlaws, and noble Indian chiefs. It happened not all that long ago in America.

Most of the Billy the Kids really were kids, armed to the teeth with cap guns and rubber-tipped arrows, staging ambushes from front porches and galloping down subur-ban streets on phantom horses.

For more than twenty years, from the 1930s straight through the 1950s, cowboy mania gripped the children of America like a high-grade fever. It started in Hollywood, where movie studios turned out Westerns faster than popped corn and radio shows invited listeners to return to the thrilling days of yesteryear. Then TV came along, and an entire generation grew up with cowboys in the living room. *The Lone Ranger*, *Hopalong Cassidy*, *The Roy Rogers & Dale Evans Show*, *Death Valley Days*, and *Have Gun—Will Travel* are just a few of the shows that made the leap from radio to television, along with new shows like *Wagon Train*, *The Rifleman*, *Rawhide*, *Maverick*, and *Bonanza*. There was hardly a night that didn't have at least one western on TV, and often more than one.

Naturally, children wanted to be just like their heroes and heroines. Requests for cowboy and cowgirl outfits, from embroidered hats to fringed vests and pint-sized

299.95
or $18 monthly

Purebred Shetlands
Have A Life Expectancy
of 25 to 30 Years

(A) PUREBRED
SHETLAND PONY

We guarantee pony to be of good conformation and perfect health. Accompanied by veterinarian's certificate of health in accordance with your state's regulations. Between 2 and 7 yrs. old, gelded and between 41 and 46-in. high at saddle. Broken, perfectly gen-tle . . . trained and ridden by children before shipment.

Choice of colors: Black and White, Solid Brown and White, Solid Black, Solid Brown or Dappled Chestnut (Spotted). You pay exp. charges. Allow 3 weeks to ship from Chicago, Ill., Columbiana, Ohio, or Leon (near Des Moines), Iowa, whichever is nearest. Shpd. at 1½ times reg. rates*, in special crate which yoursmut return at our expense. STATE: (1) No. of children in family and their ages; (2) 1st and 2nd color choice.
L94 J 1821V. Av. sh. wt. with crate 450 lbs.........299.95

The Frontier Lives Again!

FRONTIER SHERIFF'S OFFICE
- Realistic wood grain design
- "Lock-up" jail cell in back
- Tough corrugated construction

Now he can bring in the desperadoes and rustlers he captures and toss 'em in the hoosegow!

Durable corrugated jail has big "Sheriff" sign, shingled roof, wood grain effect siding. Jail office doors; 2 windows; corrugated hasp lock. Doors rigidly made of two corrugated layers with airspace in between. Gun rack in office holds weapons for "posse." Seams lock for easy assembly. Overall measurements 38x26x55 inches high. Shipping weight 12 lbs.
#35 J 4157 Mailable   2.98

Office with Lock-up
2.98

Jail "Lock-up" in back

① 2.98

③ Seminole Indian Outfit 3.98

(1) INDIAN HOLSTER SET. Two 10-in. sheep's wool holsters, leather backpieces. Plastic "beadwork" on belt and crossover straps. 8-in. repeating guns, steer head on plastic pearl handle. 6 bright 12-in. feathers on head dress, elasticized headband 1 pc. in leather belt fits up to 27-in. waists. Shpg. wt. 1 lb. 13 oz.
35 J 4198   2.98

(2) DAVY CROCKETT RIFLE and powder horn. 34-inch "Old" Betsy. High impact plastic, die-cast flintlock strikes harmless sparks. Lever for quick cocking "ammo" compartment in stock holds caps. 9-inch plastic horn with brass reed for "frontier calls." Leather thong.

④ 3.49

⑤ Outfit 2.49

boots were heard by every Santa in the land, along with sweetly innocent requests for all manner of guns and ammunition. The array of equipment was impressive as well as imaginative. There were six-shooters and Colt pistols and long-barreled affairs with ivory handles. There were single holsters and double holsters and belts adorned with flashing conchos. One belt had a silver buckle with a tiny derringer embedded in it. When the young cowboy inhaled deeply and expanded his stomach, the derringer flipped out and fired at the enemy until the scent of victory and spent caps hung heavy in the air.

SANTA'S SHOPPING LIST

Cowgirl outfit includes black skirt and bolero, both fringed and trimmed with red and white leatherette; red plaid flannel shirt; gun belt, holster, and pistol, 1944: $4.98

Embossed leather belt embellished with jewel-tone studs, with "horseshoe buckle . . . for all around smartness," 1947: $1.15

Leather gauntlets in suede finish, gold-and-white embossed cuff, fringed, 1949: $1.89

Two-tone cowboy boots with cactus pattern, 1949: $7.85

"Rodeo" Western style school bag, artificial leather trimmed with fringe, glass jewels, gold-tone buckles, and conchos, 1949: $4.98

Hopalong Cassidy socks, with Hoppy on rearing horse and Hoppy logo, 1950: 3 pairs, $1.10

"Tonto" holster set, with decorated leather holster, leather belt decorated with conchos and faux-jewels, feathered headdress, and Texas-style pistol, 1954: $3.95

Cardboard 2-room sheriff's office, 50 by 35 by 26 inches, 1954: $3.98

Lone Ranger 6-piece outfit for boys: Shirt, pants, bolo tie, chaps, holster and six-shooter, 1955: $4.79

Red cowboy hat with white trim, 1955: $1.89

Leather saddle on tripod, perfect for riding along with TV cowboys, 1955: $6.95

Shetland pony, saddle broken, trained and gentle, 1956: $299.95

LITTLE BEAUTIES

Sometime after World War II ended, a new species was spotted in America. Footloose, fancy free, and almost grownup, they roved the countryside with Dad's car keys and

money from part-time jobs in their pockets. Members of the new species, known as teenagers, changed a lot of what adults knew about the world, including just when it was that adulthood began. Girls who before the war would still have been hanging out with the crowd were putting on lipstick and going on dates. They blurred what once had been a firm line between girlhood and womanhood, and when even younger girls saw their big sisters pushing ahead, they naturally followed suit.

TV can't be blamed, but it accelerated the shortening of girlhood. When seven-year-olds saw *American Bandstand*, they started dancing like they were sixteen. When they saw *The Miss America Pageant*, they

wanted high heels and a strapless evening gown. It was no mistake that ads for "Tonette, the permanent made with the younger woman in mind" often ran during the pageant. If little girls wanted to become little women, then manufacturers would help them make the transition.

Dress up like Mommy with make-believe accessories

- Three stylish wigs
- Mock-pearl necklace
- Mock-diamond ring
- Glamorous stole
- Orchid corsage
- High-heel shoes

PLAY WIG GLAMOUR DRESS-UP KIT. Be always ready, always glamorous, for any occasion with this three-wig play set. Each wig in different hair style and color— red, blonde, brunette. For added elegance, your set includes a fully lined stole made of rayon plush that looks like the real thing. mock-pearl necklace, a ring, high-heel shoes with non-slip soles and sturdy straps. All pieces except stole are plastic.
X 921-4727 A—Shpg. wt. 2 lbs. . . . 3.99

SAVE THIS CATALOG—

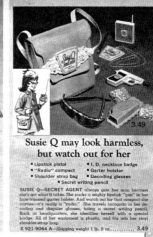

Susie Q may look harmless, but watch out for her

- Lipstick pistol
- "Radio" compact
- Shoulder strap bag
- I. D. necklace badge
- Garter holster
- Decoding glasses
- Secret writing pencil

SUSIE Q—SECRET AGENT always gets her man because she's got what it takes. She packs a mighty lipstick "gun" in her lace-trimmed garter holster. And watch out for that compact she carries—it's really a "radio." She travels incognito in her decoding and disguise glasses, toting a secret writing pencil. Back at headquarters, she identifies herself with a special badge. All of her equipment is plastic, and fits into her vinyl shoulder-strap bag.
X 921-9064 A—Shipping weight 1 lb. 8 oz. 3.49

SANTA'S SHOPPING LIST

Vanity and bench set, wood with ivory finish, 1944: $5.76

Snow White dresser set, with comb, brush, and hand mirror, decorated with scenes from the Disney movie, in a matching keepsake box, 1947: $2.69

Lady Lovely Beauty Kit, includes carrying case with mirror, play cosmetics, and accessories "so dear to feminine hearts," 1954: $1.98

Quilted pink makeup travel kit, includes a 3-section mirror, compact, hand mirror, play rouge, lipstick, comb, powder puffs, jewelry boxes, eau de cologne, and atomizer, 1955: $2.69

Glamorous accessories set with mock pearl necklace, diamond ring, fur stole, 3 wigs, high heels, and orchid corsage, 1966: $3.99

Budding Beauty French Provençal–style plastic vanity, with hassock, flip-up mirror with storage space for lipstick, soaps, bath powder, toilet water, hand lotion, bubble bath, nail polish and remover, brush, comb, hand mirror, and more, 1966: $9.88

Junior Miss Cosmetic Set, in a hatbox carrying case, includes play cosmetics, real toiletries, vanity set, manicure set, curlers, and hairpins, 1966: $1.99

2.88

4.77

3.44

1.77

1.99

3.94

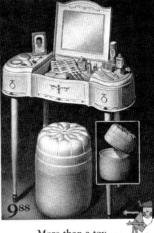

9.88

More than a toy . . .

A real vanity, sized for little ladies . . . complete with cosmetics and hassock

BUDDING BEAUTY VANITY by MARX. Made of high-impact plastic with realistic styling to add a touch of elegance to any little lady's boudoir. Under flip-up mirror is 11-pc. assortment of Tussy cosmetics for children. Includes lipstick, soaps, bath powder, toilet water, hand lotion, bubble bath, nail polish and remover, brush, comb and more. Comes with polystyrene foam hassock, storage compartment inside. Vanity measures 24x23x11 in. deep. Hassock is 12½ in. high. Semi-mailable—see page 206.
X 921-2192 A—Shipping weight 13 lbs................. 9.88

① MUSIC BOX WITH BALLERINA. Wood box covered in embossed white plastic simulated leather with dainty floral design. Open it—box plays a familiar tune while spring-mounted ballerina dances. Box is lined in rayon satin, round mirror in lid. Lots of room for little girls' trinkets, plus extra tray. Close it—snap bronze-finished luggage-type lock. Large teenage bendable doll snaps on top of box. 9x4½x3½ in. high.
X 921-9163 A—Wt. 1 lb. 4 oz. ... 4.77

② MUSIC BOX AND DOLL. Wood box covered in white plastic. Rayon satin lined. Mirror in lid. Tune plays when box opens, ballerina dances. Snap closure. Bendable doll snaps on top.
X 921-9171 A—Shpg. wt. 1 lb. ... 2.88

③ PLUSH PUPPY TISSUE DISPENSER. 21 in. long, made of rayon plush, head and legs filled with polyurethane foam. Tissues not included.
X 921-9189 A—Shpg. wt. 10 oz. ... 3.44

④ 6-PC. JUNIOR MISS VANITY SET. Dresser set in multicolor floral design on white plastic. 10½ in. hand mirror, comb, nail file, jewelry box, utility box and nylon bristle brush.
X 921-6342 A—Shpg. wt. 11 oz. ... 1.77

⑤ JUNIOR MISS 27-PC. COSMETIC SET includes everything for a lovelier little lady. Sturdy plastic hatbox with carrying handle contains mirror, brush, comb, curlers, bobby pins, 6-piece manicure set, bowl. Plus play cosmetics: perfume, hand lotion, shampoo, hair spray, 3-pc. compact set, powder, nail polish and remover, lipstick.
X 921-9197 A—Wt. 1 lb. 2 oz. ... 1.99

⑥ MARY POPPINS* HAIR DRYER. Looks just like Mommy's—blows real air! Uses 2 "D" batteries (not incl.—order on page 166). Includes dryer, hose, 2 caps, comb and brush, plastic case.
X 921-9205 A—Wt. 1 lb. 10 oz. ... 3.94

*Walt Disney Productions

3.88

Vanity and bench set . . .

■ Lift-up mirror   ■ Roomy storage compartment

JUST LIKE MOTHER'S—limed-oak-colored vanity and bench for cosmetics and accessories (not incl.—order at left). Hinged 6x8 in. lift-up mirror is cover for spacious compartment. Matching 11-inch round bench is strong enough so even Mommy can use your vanity. Sturdy corrugated fiberboard. 14½x21x27 in. Ready to assemble.
X 921-9155 A—Shipping weight 7 lbs. 8 oz. 3.88

Penneys 261

71

Come now to
WOOLWORTH'S OPEN doll HOUSE

for boxed DOLLAR-A-SET doll house furniture

It's so exciting
you'll want to play
with it yourself!

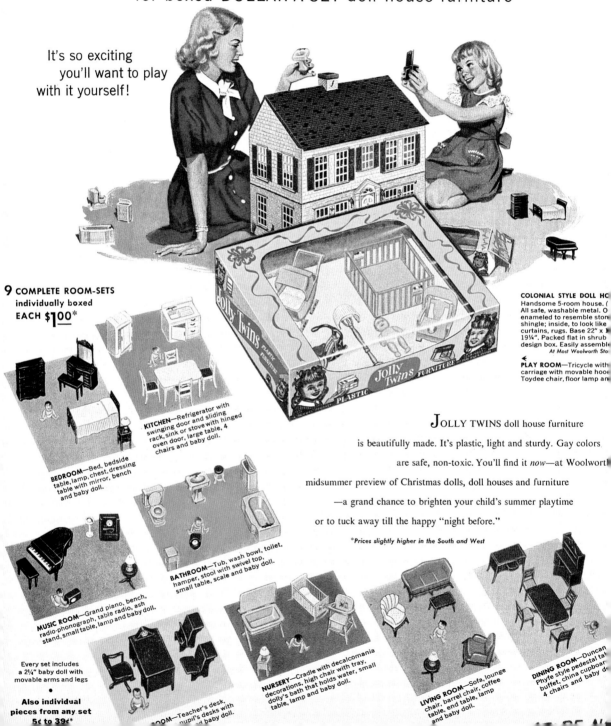

9 COMPLETE ROOM-SETS
individually boxed
EACH $1.00*

KITCHEN—Refrigerator with swinging door and sliding rack, sink or stove with hinged oven door, large table, 4 chairs and baby doll.

BEDROOM—Bed, bedside table, lamp, chest, dressing table with mirror, bench and baby doll.

BATHROOM—Tub, wash bowl, toilet, hamper, stool with swivel top, small table, scale and baby doll.

MUSIC ROOM—Grand piano, bench, radio-phonograph, table radio, ash stand, small table, lamp and baby doll.

Every set includes a 2¼" baby doll with movable arms and legs

Also individual pieces from any set 5¢ to 39¢*

...ROOM—Teacher's desk, pupil's desks with ...d baby doll.

NURSERY—Cradle with decalcomania decorations, high chair with tray, dolly's bath that holds water, small table, lamp and baby doll.

LIVING ROOM—Sofa, lounge chair, barrel chair, coffee table, end table, lamp and baby doll.

DINING ROOM—Duncan Phyfe style pedestal tab... buffet, china cupboar... 4 chairs and baby d...

COLONIAL STYLE DOLL HO...
Handsome 5-room house. (...
All safe, washable metal. O...
enameled to resemble ston...
shingle; inside, to look like...
curtains, rugs. Base 22" x ...
19¼". Packed flat in shrub...
design box. Easily assembl...
At Most Woolworth Sto...

PLAY ROOM—Tricycle with...
carriage with movable hoo...
Toydee chair, floor lamp an...

JOLLY TWINS doll house furniture
is beautifully made. It's plastic, light and sturdy. Gay colors
are safe, non-toxic. You'll find it *now*—at Woolwort...
midsummer preview of Christmas dolls, doll houses and furniture
—a grand chance to brighten your child's summer playtime
or to tuck away till the happy "night before."

*Prices slightly higher in the South and West

It's a Small, Small World

The idea of replicating the world in miniature is as old as human history, but for most of that time, those miniature worlds were part of adult activities. Often they served magical and religious purposes, and Egyptian tombs frequently held replicas of favorite possessions, pets, servants, and livestock of the deceased. Thousands of years later, kings and generals commissioned elaborate representations of battle sites, and in the days

before photography, movies, and television, three-dimensional dioramas became a popular way of displaying scenes to a mass audience. One of the most popular exhibits at the 1939 World's Fair was General Motors' Futurama, a vast section of America in which five hundred thousand miniature homes were linked by a futuristic system of highways carrying fifty thousand cars through a landscape studded

with towns, waterways, and over a million miniature trees. So large was the exhibit that visitors had to be transported over it in moving carriages.

Children loved the little worlds and models as much as adults, if not more. But the expense of making them, as well as their fragility, often made them unsuitable as toys. Still, toy makers seized whatever chance they had to make tiny things for their tiny customers. Toy soldiers and dolls that came with doll-sized cradles were early examples, but the go-small urge didn't really get rolling until the twentieth century, when cheaper methods of production and more durable materials made it possible for miniatures to become playthings. Once that happened, toy makers had a field day, knowing that when you're a very small person and almost everything and everyone is bigger than you are, holding dominion over a tiny world all your own is a very good thing indeed.

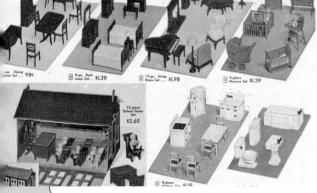

DOLLHOUSE

Like other miniature worlds, dollhouses began as display items for adults with money to burn. One of the first was made in the mid-1500s for the Duke of Bavaria, who wanted a replica of his house to put on display. The sumptuous "baby house" sparked a fad, and soon wealthy bankers and merchants across Europe were commissioning replicas of their own dwellings. The first such replicas made for children were single rooms created as teaching toys, such as the tiny kitchens that were intended to teach girls the art of household management.

Dollhouses moved firmly into the toy category in the nineteenth century but were so expensive only wealthy little girls could have them. The first attempts at mass production were cardboard affairs, with pasteboard or paper furniture pieces that were cut out and pasted together.

The modern dollhouse moved to the top of the wish list after World War II. Metal was once again available and the Depression was a thing of the

room "Happitime" Doll House . . . fully furnished

• Sears exclusive design; smartly decorated inside and out
• Sturdy fiberboard; overall size 28⅛x18x19¾ in. high $3¹⁹
• 24 pieces of fine furniture: 21 of wood, 3 of fiberboard

Your little girl's dream come true . . . a doll house with 6 big rooms plus library and den. Scenery kitchen is enclosed in the wing . . . sun deck above. Complete interior decoration lends realism seldom found in doll houses. Real looking painted-on fireplaces in living room and one bedroom; painted-on rugs and pictures. 24 pieces of furniture include: walnut-stained seaport, chair, radio, coffee table, end table and lamp for living room; table and two chairs for dining room; bed, highboy, table and lamp for each bedroom; white enameled tub, washstand and toilet for bathroom; white enameled table, fiberboard stove, refrigerator and sink for kitchen. House is very sturdy, will last for years. Available after November 1st.
'N 2105—Easy to assemble. Instructions included. Shipping weight, 4 pounds $3.19

past. Moreover, the war had shut down the German toy industry, stimulating American manufacturers to make toys that had previously been imported. By the early 1950s, the standard dollhouse was of brightly lithographed metal, with sundecks, plastic patio furniture, and attached garages that reflected a new American lifestyle. What the dollhouse lost in detail and workmanship it gained in affordability, and the toy quickly became as omnipresent under the Christmas tree as the electric train.

SANTA'S SHOPPING LIST

Pantry foods set for dollhouse with flour, corn flakes, eggs, ketchup, coffee, frozen vegetables, and potatoes, 1944: $.69

Living room set, includes sofa, club chair, barrel chair, console radio, fireplace, baby grand piano with bench, cocktail table, 2 end tables, floor lamp, and 2 table lamps, 1947: $1.98

Metal dollhouse, 1949: 5 rooms, sun deck, attached garage, fully furnished, $3.79; house with 6 rooms, sun deck, unfurnished, $3.89

Kitchen appliance set, includes toaster, waffle iron, bread board with knife and loaf of bread, mixer with mixing bowl, frying pan, pressure cooker, double boiler, griddle, coffee pot, and tea kettle, 1950: $.89

Six-room ranch-style house, metal, with cupola, weather vane, and TV antenna; comes with family of 4 and furniture for every room, 1955: $5.79

Fun, action, excitement for all youngsters

Your Choice 8⁸⁸

Fort Cheyenne! Cowboys and Indians, soldiers and horses---wagons, cannons--- all the makings of Wild West adventures!

1 **FORT CHEYENNE.** Over 270 pieces, 2 metal lithographed buildings, plastic stockade, gateway, platform, flags, wagons, cannons and shells, Indians, cowboys, soldiers, horses.
X 924-7545 A—Shipping weight 5 lbs. 4 oz............ 8.88
Similar to above, but smaller, with approximately 120 pieces.
X 924-7552 A—Shipping weight 3 lbs. 10 oz............ 4.88

YOU run your own farm! Livestock, barn, silo, equipment— fun for hours on end!

2 **FARM SET.** Over 240 pieces—all you need for doing any number of farm chores. Metal lithographed base is 13⅛x10½ in., holds a variety of metal lithographed structures with plastic roofs—open-back barn with two-story hay loft; 2 silos; chicken coop. Plastic vegetable garden has many different crops. Other plastic pieces include a large assortment of animals and farm hands, tools, mechanical equipment, fence sections.
X 924-7461 A—Shipping weight 6 lbs. 9 oz............ 8.88
Similar to above, but smaller, with 131 pieces.
X 924-7479 A—Shipping weight 4 lbs. 6 oz............ 4.88

You ARE "one of America's best"! Special Forces turn the tide of the battle— nothing stops the men of the jungle force!

3 **SPECIAL FORCES SET.** Over 323 pieces. Two opposing armies, one in olive drab, one in gray, with soldiers in many fighting positions. Highly detailed military vehicles, equipment, weapons, including pontoon, bridge, mountain, foxholes.
X 924-7560 A—Shipping weight 6 lbs............ 8.88
Similar to above, but smaller, with approximately 100 pieces.
X 924-7578 A—Shipping weight 3 lbs. 9 oz............ 4.88

Penneys 387

A WORLD IN MINIATURE

Of course, the dollhouse was just the beginning. By the 1920s, model trains began to acquire landscapes. And from the 1940s on, scaled-down worlds of every sort—with some assembly required—were likely to appear under the tree. Farms, with their fascinating entourage of machinery and animals, were especially popular. And boys loved anything that had to do with cars, from elaborate gas stations to garages to loading docks.

Frontier forts sprang up on bedroom floors across the country, and stagecoaches raced to outdistance waves of attacking Indians. In the 1950s, popular movie and TV cowboys like Roy Rogers, Hopalong Cassidy, and the Lone Ranger came out as action figures mounted on rearing or galloping horses whose detailed saddles and bridles could be taken off and put back on, along with the riders.

Toy soldiers, a popular toy for hundreds of years, enjoyed renewed popularity when they came with their own tents, barracks, and battle terrain. Sets were designed around almost every conflict imaginable, including the War of the Roses (with knights sporting lift-up visors, removable swords, and swiveling bodies), American Revolution, Civil War, Trojan War, and World War II. And just when it seemed the toy soldier might have to make way for jazzier electronic toys, a superstar parachuted onto the scene to become as famous among boys as Barbie was among girls.

THE WORLD OF G.I. JOE

In the early 1960s, the TV Western lost some of its popularity to war shows like *Combat*, *Twelve O'Clock High*, and *Hogan's Heroes*. Toy designer Stanley Weston approached Hasbro with the idea of creating a soldier figure for boys that would tap into the mood of the times. The company liked the idea of a "movable soldier" (he was *never* called a doll) and G.I. Joe debuted at the 1964 Toy Fair. Standing eleven and a half inches tall, with twenty-one articulated parts and a battle scar on his face, he was like nothing else the toy world had ever seen. Boys loved him, not only because he was a rough, tough, hero, but also because his inventors created enough accessories to make Barbie pea green with envy. The accessory sets, for every mission conceivable, were meticulously detailed and impressively authentic-looking. His astronaut suit, of silver metallic fabric, came with a realistic helmet, watertight space capsule "designed from 'Mercury Control' plans," and recording of a Gemini flight. A frogman unit came with a scuba suit, fins, mask, and battery-powered sea sled that could glide atop the water or dive below it.

By Christmas of 1964, there was an official G.I. Joe fan club, and the action hero was one of the season's best-selling toys. So great was his presence that few people realize the original figure was made for just four years, though attempts were made to bring him back in different sizes. By 1968, with the shadow of Vietnam casting a pall over the country, the popularity of war toys was definitely in decline. But, as General MacArthur said, old soldiers never die, and the memory of G.I. Joe burns bright to this very day.

SANTA'S SHOPPING LIST

Deluxe farm set, with heavy cardboard buildings that include farmhouse, barn, horse barn, brooder, silo, tool shed, dog house, windmill, 18 fence pieces, 5 trees, tractor, plow, wagon and automobile; molded "wood-plastic" animals include 4 chickens, rooster, cow, calf, pig, 2 piglets, turkey, colt, and dog, 1944: $2.89

One-room cardboard schoolhouse, with plastic pieces, includes 6 movable desks and 4 students, teacher's desk with moving drawers and swivel chair, 1947: $2.69

Supermarket with large window, door that opens, and striped awning that can be raised or lowered, interior with dairy case, frozen foods case, meat counter, turnstile, cash register, and shelves lined with brand-name groceries, 1947: $3.98

Two-story lithographed steel gas station, with working car elevator, ramp from rooftop parking lot to ground level, working gas pumps with hoses that squirt water, 1949: $4.45

Fire station with siren, doors that go up and down, pump engine with hose that can be filled from the included hydrant, 2 "burning" buildings, ladder truck with extendable ladder, and fire chief's car, 1949: $4.49

Army Training Center, comes with lithographed metal headquarters building furnished with desk, swivel chair, switchboard, rifle rack, map table, file cabinet, waste basket, bench, and chairs; also includes 100 plastic soldiers in marching as well as combat positions, fencing, tents, machine guns, mounted bazookas, flags, trees, rocks, scout cars, and half track, 1950: $5.98

Plasticville, U.S.A. rural unit with house, barn, bridge, pond, trees, fencing, well, barbecue, farm animals, and outhouse, 1954: $4.95

King Arthur castle set, with walled castle courtyard that has turrets and working drawbridge, 20 plastic knights with movable banners, swords, shields, and lances; 6 horses dressed for battle, and 3 cannons that shoot plastic balls, 1955: $4.79

Super Circus set, lithographed metal big top has 3 rings and is flanked by 2 midway sections, includes ringmaster, acrobats, trapeze artists, animal tamers, jugglers, clowns, vendors, lions, giraffes, camels, monkeys, seals, elephants, tigers, leopards, and alligators, 1955: $3.98

G.I. Joe with basic Army, Navy, Marine, or Air Force uniform and equipment, 1965: $1.98

G.I. Joe motorcycle with sidecar, 1965: $3.33

G.I. Joe Marine beachhead tent set, 1965: $2.98

Johnny West, cowboy, 11 ½ inches tall, jointed to stand, squat, and shoot, comes with plastic rifle, six-shooter, pistol, knife, chaps, spurs, hat, gun belt and holster, branding irons, canteen, and cookout set that includes grate, coffee pot, tin cup, and frying pan, 1966: $2.66

Thunderbolt, Johnny West's horse, tan with cream markings, comes with plastic sadle, bridle, saddle blanket, saddlebags, rifle, and holster, 1966: $1.99

Mattel three-tier space station with battery-powered flashing radar beacon and solar panels on top tier, 1966: $8.97

Space station's Captain Lazer, includes light-up laser pistol, radiation shield, cosmic beacon, and paralyzer wand, 1966: $5.87

Fort Independence, stockade with 4 block houses, ladders, fences, gate, house with chimney, 2 lean-tos, flags, cannon, covered wagon, horses, 16 cowboys, and 16 Indians, 1969: $13.99

Cape Kennedy set includes working gantry that takes 7 astronauts up to the nose cone, tower with revolving radar, loading crane, supply truck, 4 firing missiles, helicopter, rocket that really launches, 1966: $3.67

Three-story parking garage with gas station, has working elevator, car ramp from roof to road, pump meter that registers gallons, light up Shell sign and cars, batteries not included, 1969: $9.99

WE BUILT THIS CITY

Of course, if you didn't like the small worlds on offer from Santa's workshop, you could always ask for a toy to help you make your own. The first construction toy to arrive on the scene was the modernistic-looking Erector Set, invented by twenty-eight-year-old Alfred Carlton Gilbert in 1912. After watching railroad workers erect steel girders, Gilbert streamlined and miniaturized the system. Heralded as an educational toy that would help boys learn engineering principles, the Erector Set was first toy ever to have its own ad campaign. "Hello, boys! Make lots of toys!" the tag line went. Sales were so impressive that the Erector Set became the flagship product for a whole company and A. C. Gilbert went on to create other learning-based items like a chemistry set and home microscope. He also began to offer larger, more complex Erector Sets, which came with motors, engines, gears, and pulleys that allowed youngsters to create Ferris wheels, zeppelins, and steam shovels.

Just a year after the Erector Set debuted, another construction toy came along. This one was inspired by children themselves, whose play with pencils, thread spools, and sticks prompted Charles Pajeau and Robert Petit to create Tinkertoys. Sets originally sold for sixty cents and were packaged in a durable cardboard cylinder for easy mailing. The toy was a smash-hit with youngsters, and more than three million sets were sold over the next five years. Although the basic pieces did not change in their design, sets became larger and more elaborate. Red spools were added in 1932, and sticks appeared in red, green, blue, and yellow in the 1950s. The addition of red cardboard blades allowed builders to experiment with windmills and whirligigs.

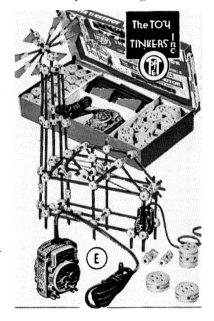

The next building craze to sweep the junior set was a fanciful step backward in time. Designed by Frank Lloyd Wright's son, John, it consisted of chunky, down-to-earth miniature redwood logs that interlocked for a sturdy fit. Named Lincoln Logs, they were marketed as a toy that typified the resourceful, do-it-yourself spirit of America. The 1924 debut

was fortunate, for Westerns soon became a staple of the growing film industry, triggering a nostalgic romance with America's pioneer past. Although the little logs reached their highest popularity during the Davy Crockett craze of the 1950s, they won fans in every generation and were selling over a hundred million sets worldwide by the end of the century.

Just as the frontier craze was beginning to quiet down, a new and completely different building system came along. Created in Denmark and imported to the U.S. in 1958, the new toy seemed a perfect mirror of the era. For one thing, pieces weren't wood or metal—they were plastic. They were also made of bright, multicolored, and seemingly indestructible plastic. Best of all, they were simultaneously simple, complex, and versatile. Just three of the eight-stud bricks, in

the same color, could be put together 1,560 different ways. Six would yield 102,981,504 combinations. The little bricks were easy to put together, and so precisely molded that they did not come apart until deliberately dismantled. In fact, the only problem children had with Legos was that grown-ups just couldn't keep their hands off them. Adults ended up loving the toy almost as much as children and have devoted hours to building enormous and complex structures all around the world. Legos have been sighted in the form of the Loch Ness monster (at Florida's Disney World), as a replica of the Chrysler Building (in the Times Square Toys "Я" Us store in New York), and dozens of other structures around the world. In fact, it's estimated that there are fifty-two Lego pieces for every human being on the planet. Fortune magazine named it the toy of the twentieth century.

SANTA'S SHOPPING LIST

Tinkertoys, 1944: 81-piece set, $.55; 126-piece set, $1.05; 190-piece set, $1.79

Interlocking wood blocks that resemble real bricks when hooked together to make buildings, includes doors, windows, and roof pieces, 1949: 100-piece set, $.89; 200-piece set, $1.75, 400-piece set, $3.49; 600-piece set, $5.45

Lincoln Logs "of seasoned hardwood. stained brown to resemble rough hewn logs," deluxe 334-piece set, 1944: $4.25

Transogram Construct-All set with plastic girders to assemble, includes "Riv-A-Matic" gun and remote-control motor, 1966: $14.44

Gilbert All-Electric Erector set in metal case, includes 110-volt engine, pieces, and instructions to make items like working Ferris wheel, windmill, and drawbridge, 1949: $19.95

American Plastic Bricks, interlocking bright red bricks, white foundation blocks, doors, windows, and green roof pieces, 1954: 208-piece set, $3.50

Master Tinkertoy set with 3-speed motor, 1954: $9.85

Lego Master Builder set, with bricks, 4 sizes gears, wheels, and accessories, 1969: $15.99

Where All the Children Are Above Average

It goes without saying: *all* children are above average, and every parent knows it. With the massive improvements of the twentieth century, such as public education and a standard of living that made child labor a thing of the past, parents finally had the opportunity to send Billy and Susie out there to prove them right. Schools developed sophisticated arts programs and the lessons industry boomed. There were after-school music lessons and Saturday-morning classes in tap, ballet, acrobatics, and baton. And, of course, there were toys—toys that taught 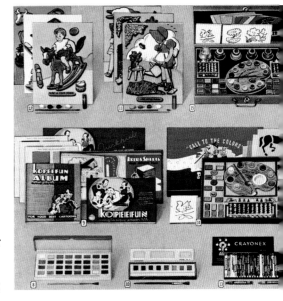 musical scales, toys that promised drawing skills, toys for budding scientists and architects-in-the-making. There were toys for every talent imaginable, and some even Mom and Dad *hadn't* imagined.

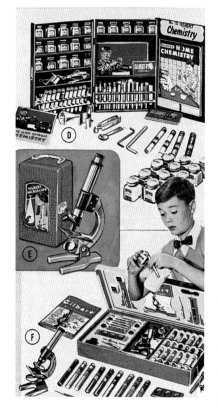

THE MAD SCIENTIST IN US ALL

No sooner had World War II ended than the Cold War began, and with it a quiet but pervasive understanding that technology was the key to beating the Russians. A TV show called *Watch Mr. Wizard* featured a likeable host, Don Herbert, leading boys and girls through science experiments that were unquestionably cool. Fanciful shows, like the space adventure *Captain Video*, and the real race to put a man in orbit upped the interest. The A.C. Gilbert Company, which specialized in science-oriented toys as well as Erector Sets, sold thousands of microscopes and chemistry sets. In 1960, as America counted down to its first manned space flight, Gilbert reported that sales of astronomy kits were up 25 percent over the previous year. Not that all eyes were on the heavens—that same year, the hot Christmas toy was the Visible Man, an assemble-it-yourself kit of bones and organs to paint and fit into a transparent body traced with red and blue arteries and veins. The Visible Man was soon followed by the even more interesting Visible Woman, who could be converted to a visible mother-to-be with the aid of a plastic fetus.

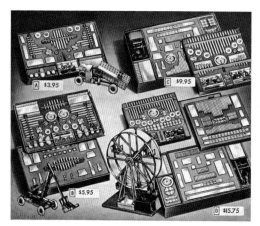

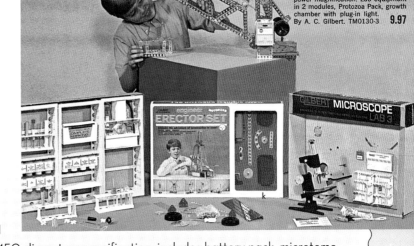

(l) **MICROSCOPE LAB 3** has Zoom microscope with 75, 250 and 500 power magnification. Lab equipment in 2 modules, Protozoa Pack, growth chamber with plug-in light. By A. C. Gilbert. TM0130-3   **9.97**

SANTA'S SHOPPING LIST

Gilbert Junior Laboratory chemistry set in a hinged metal box, includes chemicals, test tubes, alcohol lamps, filter, litmus paper, manual and booklet with instructions for 223 experiments, 1949: $3.50; Senior set, capable of 381 experiments, $7.95

Gilbert microscope in hinged wooden cabinet with up to 450-diameter magnification, includes battery pack, microtome, dissecting equipment, specimen pan, chemicals, stains, specimens, slides, test tubes, rack, and instruction book, 1949: $10.95

It even has real URANIUM ORE specimens.

— Sears Christmas catalog, 1950

Deluxe Senior Chemistry Set with "new atomic energy feature" and enough chemicals and equipment to perform over 600 experiments, 1950: $11.25

Harmonic Reed Spitz Jr. Planetarium projects stars and constellations on the walls or ceiling, adjustable to show the sky as it would appear from anywhere on the globe during any month, with rheostat to control light intensity, 1954: $14.95

Transistor Radio Kit, includes pre-assembled cabinet, tuner, headphones, diode detector and transistor amplifier, 1966: $7.98

Digicomp I Computer Kit makes a plastic computer that can add, subtract, multiply, divide and be programmed to solve more complex programs, 1966: $5.98

Geology Lab, comes with pick, alcohol lamp, jolly balance, magnifying glass, streak plate, 20 rock specimens, chemicals, test tubes, rack, and more, 1969: $8.99

Visible Man or Visible Woman, kits for transparent human figures that reveal organs inside the body; Visible Woman comes with 7-month fetus, 1969: $4.88 each

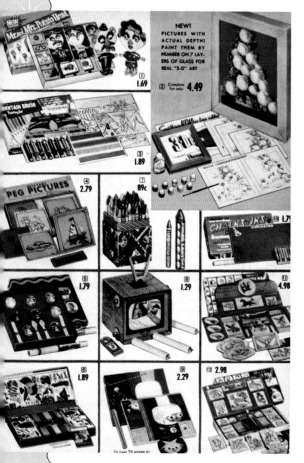

NEW!
PICTURES WITH
ACTUAL DEPTH!
PAINT THEM BY
NUMBER ON 7 LAY-
ERS OF GLASS FOR
REAL "3-D" ART

FOR THE LITTLE ARTIST

Finger paints were just the beginning. And that little box of eight watercolors? Strictly for amateurs! The modern child was a *gifted* child, just itching to get in touch with his or her inner Picasso. Would the toy industry fail to offer the means to do so? Not on your life. The box of eight Crayolas that debuted for a nickel in 1903 mushroomed to forty-eight in 1949, grew to sixty-four in 1958, and achieved a glorious seventy-two in the early '70s. Paint sets came with dozens of colors, mixing palettes, and an assortment of brushes.

There were even new ways to create art. In 1960, a toy came along that looked exactly like a toy children already loved—television. With its cheerful red frame, gray screen, and turning knobs, the Etch A Sketch resembled a private, portable TV. Children couldn't resist doodling, and parents appreciated a toy that was so blissfully mess free. For those of you who've always wondered how it worked but never had the nerve to take it apart, here's the scoop: the inside compartment of the Etch A Sketch is filled with a very fine, highly adherent aluminum powder that will stick to anything and everything (a good reason never to deconstruct the toy). When the case is turned upside down and shaken, the powder completely coats the screen. The design is made by a small stylus mounted on the intersection of two rods, one horizontal and one vertical. The knobs move the rods, and the stylus traces a line in the aluminum powder.

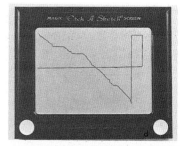

(d) **ETCH A SKETCH** is loads of fun for boys, girls and everyone. Just turn the knobs and create thousands of designs. No paper, no pencils, no mess! Shake to erase. Just "etch a sketch." TD0576-4 **2.44**

Five years after the Etch A Sketch, an English mechanical engineer invented a toy that allowed even the artistically challenged to make beautifully intricate patterns by fitting a small disk to a pen and placing it within a larger wheel. Kenner bought rights to manufacture the toy and the Spirograph made its debut in 1965. It was a best-seller that Christmas and the following Christmas as well. Within two years, over 5.5 million sets had sold—the ability to create such complex art so effortlessly was just too much to resist.

SANTA'S SHOPPING LIST

Giant 193-piece paint set with 6 jars poster paint, 72 cake water colors, 16 crayons, 2 brushes, palette, 10 stencils, 81 pictures to paint, and a color chart, 1947: $1.92

Stampee Stamp set with 10 rubber stamps of farm and zoo animals, stamp pad, crayons, and instructions, 1947: $.89

Electric etching pencil with an assortment of foils and emery cloth; create your own designs or order extra pre-marked plaques, 1949: $1.79

Young artist's easel with shaded light, liquid water colors, mixing pan, crayons, chalk, and large roll of paper, 1950: $3.98

Colorama set includes perforated board and 10 boxes of colored beads to create mosaic-like pictures, 1954: $2.50

Craft Master paint-by-numbers oil painting set, "no lessons needed," 1954: $3.50

Ungar Wood Burning Set with electric pencil, 8 wood plaques, 6 sheets of embossing foil, paints, and brushes, 1955: $5

Etch A Sketch, "Just turn the knobs and create thousands of designs," 1966: $2.44

Spirograph, with 2 wheels, 22 design rings, 4 pens, paper, tray, baseboard, and instructions, 1969: $2.99

Lite-Brite, plug it in, put the pegs in the board and create colorful moving pictures, comes with movement lever, 2 plastic screens, 400 pegs in 8 colors, cord, and picture sheets, 1969: $6.66

A

B

C

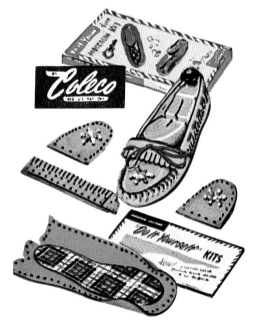

Walco

D

Walco INDIAN BEADCRAFT

I MADE IT MYSELF!

Americans have always been resourceful. Weaving baskets. Making their own buckskins. Sewing quilts out of cast-off scraps. Landing in a howling wilderness made do-it-yourself projects more or less a necessity. Somewhere along the line, though, necessity morphed into crafting. The drive to make it yourself runs deep, and the craftmania of today is no surprise to anyone who remembers the Christmas toys of yesteryear. Ironically, while many crafts are thought of as feminine concerns, one of the most successful craft toys of all times was beloved almost exclusively by boys.

CREEPY CRAWLERS THINGKMAKER

What the Easy Bake Oven was to girls, Mattel's Creepy Crawlers Thingmaker was to boys. It debuted in 1964 and it was clear from the very beginning that it had almost everything a boy could want. There was an exciting substance called Plastigoop that, when poured into molds and baked in the Thingmaker, produced battalions of spiders, worms, and bugs guaranteed to make Mom turn pale. To this day, grown men are likely to remember it as their all-time favorite toy and wax nostalgic about the smell of the solidifying goop and the sheer excitement of having a toy that heated up enough to bake bread or melt a carpet. The original set was soon supplemented by sets that made all sorts of things, such as Fighting Men and Creeple Peeple in 1965. A Fun Flowers set was introduced to appeal to girls in 1966, but later that year—just in time for Halloween and Christmas—Mattel restored boys' faith with the Fright Factory, a deliciously gross and ghoulish collection of scars, eyeballs, shrunken heads and other oddities. Though the toy has passed through the hands of several manufacturers, it remains in production today, with new molds added from time to time. Apparently, as long as children love goo, there will be Thingmakers—and that's forever.

Our Thingmakers® make things.
(Like Creepy Crawlers, Creeple Peeple, Fighting Men.)

A year ago, we invented the Creepy Crawlers *Thingmaker®*. Now millions of boys and girls are making Creepy Crawlers, playing with Creepy Crawlers, even selling Creepy Crawlers.

This year, we've got two new Thingmakers. One makes Creeple Peeple. They're kind of ugly, but lovable. And fun to wear, or stick on the end of a pencil.

The other Thingmaker makes Fighting Men: whole armies of toy soldiers, and all their equipment.

There's just one problem. We can't figure out whether kids have more fun making toys with our Thingmakers, or playing with the toys they've made.

ker

R" is the registered trademark of Mattel, Inc.,
CASTING UNIT AND MATERIALS.

Creeple Peeple

Creepy Crawlers

Fighting Men

SANTA'S SHOPPING LIST

Raffia basket-weaving kit, makes 8 baskets, 4 to 6 inches in diameter, 1944: $1.06

Sea Shell Jewelry kit, comes with "hundreds of sea shells and beads" ready to be strung into necklaces, bracelets, and decorations, as well as needles, cord, awls, and complete instructions, 1947: $2.95

Model Craft Walt Disney set with everything needed to make plaster models of favorite Disney characters, including rubber molds, molding powder, mixing bowl, paints and brush, 1949: $2.65

Big Charm Craft jewelry kit, comes with chains, clasps, plastic beads, and over 50 charms to make bracelets, necklaces and earrings, 1950: $2.29

Hardwood handloom "weaves beautiful fabric in endless variety of patterns," comes with 3 skeins yarn and 3 plastic shuttles, 1950: $5.59

Leatherworking kit for making a billfold, comb case, and coin purse, 1950: $1.08

Creative Metal Tapping Kit, comes with colored metal plaques with wood bases, tapping hammer, punch, mounting nails, sandpaper, sanding block and instruction book to make 7 embossed plaques, 1954: $2

Build-your-own White House kit with 16-inch lithographed base, building pieces, accessories, adhesive, and instructions, 1954: $2.98

Leather Indian moccasin kit with precut pieces for beaded moccasins, air-foam insoles, lacings, and instructions, 1954: $1.98

Lisbeth Whiting Perfume Kit contains large flask of perfume base, 5 vials of scent to mix, funnel, eye dropper, 96 "clever bottle labels," and instructions, 1954: $3

Indian beadcraft by Walco for making belts and bracelets in an "authentic Indian design," includes loom, wires, needles, thread, 10 vials of seed beads, and instructions, 1955: $2.50

Costume jewelry craft kit with sequins, spangles, beads, simulated

Smart, colorful costume jewelry for every season of the year can be made with this fine set.

The Toy Yearbook, 1954–1955

pearls, rhinestones, and findings for earrings, necklaces, and bracelets, 1955: $3; Pearl jewelry craft kit, $2.50

Loom, replica of professional floor model, can weave pieces up to 8 inches wide, comes with shuttles, yarn, and instructions, 1966: $5.99

Creepy Crawlers Thingmaker, with heating unit, molds, 4 bottles of Plastigoop (red, yellow, black, and green) and everything else needed to make over 30 different kinds of snakes, spiders, and bugs, 1966: $6.99

Plastigoop refills, in red, yellow, black, green, fluorescent green, fluorescent blue, fluorescent pink, or fluorescent orange, 2-ounce bottle, 1966: $1.39

Power Mite kit, with balsa wood, styrofoam, and plans for projects like birdhouses and toy sailboats, for use with Power Mite tools, 1969: $3.19; Power Mite battery-powered tool line includes drill, circular saw, sander, and router, 1969: $2.99 each

Suede leather purse kit, makes fringed shoulder bag, 1969: $5.99

Everything for the Junior Carpenter!
Power Mite Workbench, two Battery-Operated Mini Tools, Hand-Tools, and Pegboard!

[1] **POWER MITE WORKSHOP!** Workbench has hinged top—opens to storage space. Power for tools supplied by externally mounted receptacle. Peg-board secures tools. Includes: sabre saw, drill, square, hammer, screwdriver, C-clamp, bench vise, wrench, blueprints, balsa wood, styrofoam. Bench 11x3¼x9 in. high. Uses 2 D-cell batteries (not included—order below item [5]).
X 924-5002 A—Mail. wt. 3.70 lbs. 8.88

POWER MITE MATERIALS KIT. Contains a generous supply of styrofoam and balsa wood of thickness suitable for Power Mite tools, together with a set of plans.
X 923-5748 A—Mail. wt. 0.10 lb. 3.19

[2] to [5] **POWER MITE MINI TOOLS.** Miniature-sized plastic tools—look like the one dad uses! Each of the four tools can drill or cut through balsa wood and styrofoam. Hinged carrying case serves as battery housing and plug-in connection for each miniature tool. Operate on 2 D-cell batteries (not included—order below).

[2] Drill With Case. Includes 3 interchangeable bits.
X 924-5267 A—Wt. 0.90 lb. 2.99

[3] Circular Saw With Case. Includes extra blade.
X 924-5374 A—Wt. 0.90 lb. 2.99

[4] Router With Case. Includes 3 cutters.
X 923-5706 A—Wt. 0.75 lb. 2.99

[5] Sander With Case. Includes extra sandpaper.
X 924-5358 A—Wt. 0.90 lb. 2.99

D-cell Batteries. Pkg. of 6. 1.25 lbs.
X 957-1761 A .... Order 1 pkg. for 99c

76 TROMBONES — AND A LOT OF ACHING EAR DRUMS

A lot of things happened in 1957. The Russians put Sputnik into orbit. The word *beatnik* came into use for the first time. *Leave It To Beaver* and *American Bandstand* hit the airwaves while *West Side Story* and *The Music Man* opened on Broadway. And music—or what passed for music—could be heard across the land.

According to *Time* magazine, eight million school children were playing musical instruments in school, and more were taking lessons on their own time. Sales of electronic organs had risen 600 percent since 1952, prompting an understandably gleeful Stanley Sorenson, president of Hammond, to assure *Time*'s reporter, "If you can get it in the house, you can sell it."

It was all part of the Talented Child Syndrome, and things had been moving toward this crescendo for years. Parents insisted on far more than the three R's for their children. They wanted singing and dancing as well. By the time children reached the upper elementary grades and were offered music lessons as an elective, the idea of picking up a flute or a coronet didn't seem strange or daunting at all. They'd been playing instruments for years, toy ones.

SANTA'S SHOPPING LIST

Student xylophone by Silvertone with chromium plated steel bars, 2 octave range, 1947: $32.50

Silvertone professional harmonica, 1947: $1.89

Easy-to-play plastic bagpipes, 1950: $5.29

Baby grand piano with bench, 3 full octaves, top that raises, modeled after real concert models, 1950: $37.50

Melodé Bells Swiss-style bells in color-coded plastic, set of 8, with music book, 1954: $4.98

Emenee musical instruments, in plastic with gold or silver metallic finish, each with musical instruction book and carrying case, 1954: saxophone, $6; tuba, $15; trumpet, clarinet, or glockenspiel, $4; trombone, $7

It's accepted by the kids now. In my day it was considered sissy.

— Music teacher, quoted in *Time* magazine, 1957

Electric guitar "with the new 'coot' look" and nylon and wire strings, amplifier included, 1966: $13.88

Snare drum set comes with tom-tom drum, brass cymbal, cow bell, wire brushes, drumsticks, drum stand and instruction book, 1966: $29.88

2-octave zither, with song charts, 1969: $7.77

3-octave electric table organ, with 12 chord buttons, 1969: $27.88

"O-OH-H DAD! ...It's a SCHWINN!"

The famous SCHWINN PHANTOM—glistening with more beauty, studded with special features—the finest bicycle in America today!

SCHWINN EXCLUSIVE QUALITY FEATURES
FOR EXTRA VALUE ... EXTRA PLEASURE

✓ **EXCLUSIVE SCHWINN "LOOK"**—Smartly designed, richly finished, Schwinn Bicycles are outstanding for beauty. Each evidences Schwinn's long experience.

✓ **EXCLUSIVE ELECTRO-FORGED FRAME**—Schwinn's own process makes it one continuous steel structure ... safest, most durable bicycle frame ever built.

✓ **EXCLUSIVE "DUR-A-ROL" BEARINGS**—Roll easier, last longer. They make possible the effortless pedaling for which Schwinn Bicycles are famous.

✓ **EXCLUSIVE TUBULAR RIMS**—Special Schwinn construction. Lighter, yet 5-times more rigid than ordinary rims. Built to withstand abuse!

✓ **EXCLUSIVE FRONT HUB**—Schwinn-made for longer life and easier rolling. Bearings triple-heat-treated for extra-durability.

America's Favorite Bicycles 9 t

This Christmas, Schwinn Bicycles are more than ever the with boys and girls ... preferred 9 to 1 over any other

Your youngster's joy is bound to be greater when the bike y a Schwinn ... because Schwinn is the bike every child wants. Schwinn Bicycles, with their beautiful colors and many specia so loved by children, are the *preferred* make by far.

The Schwinn name means *quality*—for into these bicycl finest materials and the skill of the Schwinn family's 70 yea tinuous experience. Schwinn Bicycles are built for extra-safety, *last* ... and backed by a written guarantee that's *honored to*

You'll find one of the 12,000 Schwinn Authorized Dealers Have him show you today why a Schwinn Bicycle gives mo for-dollar value. Schwinns come in every price class—delivere *ride*. For the best Christmas your youngster ever had—*give a*

Take That Thing Outside:

OUTDOOR TOYS

In a world of constant change, where parents have been told since the time of Socrates that their children are going to the dogs, it's reassuring to remember that the favorite new outdoor toys were also the favorite *old* outdoor toys, and many have been around longer than Christmas itself. The first sled was probably invented by a prehistoric child who decided the shoulder blade of a woolly mammoth would be a pretty good thing to slide down a hill on. Skis and ice skates have also been around a long time. Roller skates were first glimpsed on a London stage in the 1740s, and the first pair that used two sets of side-by-side wheels was designed in New York at the start of the Civil War. They proved so popular that a public rink opened a few years later. Although roller skating is largely thought of as a solo sport today, for young people of past decades it was as popular on dates as dancing.

Red Riders for Junior Citizens

But for something new and shiny under the tree, nothing beat the bicycle. To a child, a bicycle meant power and a heady sort of freedom generally reserved for adults. With a bicycle you could go anywhere, even beyond the call of Mom's summoning voice. And even if you had to wait until the snow melted and the weather cleared, it was sitting there waiting, like a giant promise with a bow on it. The first bicycles came without pedals. To propel them, the rider had to push along with his feet. Not until pedals were added in the 1860s did bicycles become truly popular.

The early bicycle was front-wheel-drive only. The rear wheel, which was often smaller than the front, was simply there for balance. The bikes were a primative affair, called "bone shakers" for a good reason, and women in their long, confining skirts had no hope of peddling fast enough to maintain balance. For them, the tricycle made its first appearance, with a smaller front wheel and rear wheels as tall as the rider's seat. The big breakthrough came with the invention of stronger, lighter, more flexible metals and the addition of a sprocket chain that allowed power to be drawn from both wheels. The modern bicycle was born.

Bicycles designed especially for children began to be marketed just after the First World War. Sized for growing bodies and altogether flashier than adult models, they were an instant hit. The metal and rubber shortages of World War II made hopes of a new bicycle all but impossible for most children of the time. Black marketeers sold shoddy, secondhand machines that went for as much as sixty dollars, and even a new model that sold legally—if you were lucky enough to get one—was luxury-priced. When the war ended and shortages finally eased, bicycles became one of the best-selling, most enduringly popular toys of the twentieth century.

NEW TOYS ON THE BLOCK

Of course, there were new toys invented for outdoor play. One of the first, the Pogo Stick, came along in 1919 and became one of the hottest fads of the Roaring Twenties. Jumping contests were held, and Pogo-loving couples exchanged vows on them. George Hansburg, who invented the toy after watching a Burmese girl playing with a flexible bamboo pole, taught the ladies of the Ziegfeld Follies to Pogo, and the chorus girls of the New York Hippodrome performed entire routines on them.

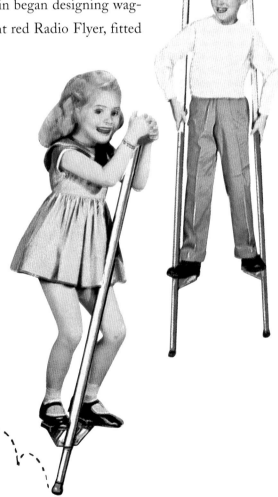

Wagons and small carts for children, often pulled by dogs, ponies, and even turkeys, were not new, but in 1923 a young Italian immigrant named Antonio Pasin began designing wagons for urban use. Eventually his bright red Radio Flyer, fitted with sturdy wheels and a handle for pulling, became *the* quintessential child's wagon. Asked about the curious name, Pasin explained that he liked to give his inventions titles that captured the spirit of the times, and Radio Flyer came about at a time when everyone was mesmerized by the fascinating new wireless invention, the radio, that sent words flying at the speed of sound.

Pedal cars became especially popular in the 1950s, taking all manner of fanciful shapes, from Cadillacs to fire trucks to planes and even rocket ships.

For older boys, sports equipment was popular. Prior to the 1950s, most driveways were dirt, gravel, or brick, while lawns were swathes of unbroken

Merry Christmas for Your Boy

green. But in the new, seemingly endless tracts of housing known as suburbs, the family yard was reconfigured. Driveways were paved with blacktop or cement, and large patios were likely to be found out back. Children could skate in their own driveways and play basketball at home. Swing sets, tetherballs, badminton nets, and even trampolines sprang up like clover in America's backyards. Kids had been building their own skate boards for years, and in 1958 adults finally caught on and began manufacturing and selling commercial models.

The same year the first skateboard was manufactured, along came a lightweight wonder, a simple large ring of tubular hard plastic that triggered the first mass fad of the space age. Swung around the waist or hips and kept in orbit, the new toy from Wham-O could do a amazing amount of damage to ornaments if the user stood too near the Christmas tree. Most Hula Hoops were instantly banished to the backyard or playroom, but it wasn't long before Mom or Dad snuck down to try their own luck. There was a knack to Hula Hooping, and those really adept at it could keep multiple rings going at once. Like the Pogo Stick of the 1920s, Hula Hoops were an enormous fad, complete with contests, world records, and musical routines. Over a hundred million of them had been sold by 1960, and factories were soon turning them out at the rate of twenty thousand a day.

Sporting Toys...Sure to Make a

LET'S GO SHOPPING!

Croquet set for four, 1945: $5.99

Striped canvas teepee-style tent with awning, poles and stakes included, 5 feet tall, 56 inches square, 1945: $6.39

Leather baseball glove, 1945: $5.39

Leather boxing gloves for young boys, padded and lined, 1947: $5.98

Scooter, red enamel over steel, 1947: $3.95

Hook and ladder fire truck pedal car, 1947: $17.95

Flying Arrow sled, wood with steel frame and runners, 46 inches long, 1947: $4.69

Archery set with target on tripod-stand, bow, and 4 arrows with suction-cup tips, 1949: $2.95

Radio Flyer wagon, 1950: $7.29

Pogo Stick, 1954: $6.95

Stilts, adjustible to 21 inches off the ground, 1954: $4.95

Fishing set, rod, reel, line, leader, bobber, fish stringer, tackle box with hooks and sinkers, 1955: $5.98

Roadmaster bicycle, 16" wheels, with removable training wheels, 1955: $27.95

Roller skates, leather strap, clamp-on style, with key, nickel plated, 1957: $3.00

Hula Hoop, 1960: $1

Battery-powered go-kart, by Marx, 1960: $30

Tubular steel frame bicycle, with horn, headlight, and flashing tail light, girls' or boys' model, 1966: $48.88

Girls' or boys' figure skates, flannel lined, 1966: $7.88

Regulation-style football, with kicking tee, 1967: $4.98

Six Can't-Be-Categorized Classics

Of course, there are always some toys that defy classification. Here are six of the most memorable.

COLORFORMS: The original 1951 Colorforms—brightly colored, geometric vinyl shapes that would cling to a shiny cardboard canvas—were clearly an art toy. A child could use the shapes to build pictures of things like houses and flowers or to create Mondriaan-like abstracts. The line soon expanded, with sets that functioned as every thing from teaching toy paper dolls to a kind of do-it-yourself comic book. Popeye became the first licensed Colorforms character set in 1957, followed by everything from Disney's *101 Dalmations* to Malibu Barbie. There were sets that taught numbers and

letters, and sets that let children experiment with fashion and clothing combinations. No matter what shape they came in—and there were thousands—children always loved them and still do today.

MR. MACHINE: He seemed the poster boy for impersonal science toys, a wind-up robot whose gears could be observed as he rolled across the floor. The amazing thing was that the little fellow with the memorable grin, red plastic head, arms, and legs, with a big blue wind-up key at his back and a snub nose made of a white plastic screw was *lovable*. Even girls loved him, and girls weren't supposed to like mechanical gizmos. Debuting in 1961 and priced at twelve dollars, he shot straight to the top of Christmas wish lists. His name, proudly emblazoned on his red plastic top hat, comes from his creator, inventor Marvin Glass, whose wife once kidded him that he turned out new toy ideas at such a pace he was a regular "Mr. Machine."

MR. POTATO HEAD: When the admonition to "Eat your vegetables" didn't seem enough, designer George Lerner created a set of silly facial features to make vegetables look a bit friendlier. Intended as giveaways in cereal boxes, the Hasbro company bought the product and turned it into a toy. The original 1952 Mr. Potato Head appeared as a twenty-eight-piece set that included various eyes, noses, mouths, and ears. The toy was one of the first ever advertised on television, a stroke of genius that led to sales topping four million dollars in just a few months. The next year, Mr. Potato Head acquired a wife, and Mr. and Mrs. Potato Head settled down to enjoy a long run of success. The molded plastic bodies didn't come along until 1964. Before that, you had to supply your own potato.

ROCK 'EM SOCK 'EM ROBOTS: Were they dolls? A game? A toy? A preview of the joystick-based video games to come? The two robots, named the Red Rocker and the Blue Bomber and colored accordingly, went at it in a miniature boxing ring, their slugging action controlled by a pair of joy-sticks. Boys loved the game because, if you got the action just right, your robot could cause his opponent's head to fly off. In fact, most people who loved the toy remember it best for the tagline: "Knock his block off!"

ROCKING HORSE: Rocking horses began appearing in nurseries sometime in the 1500s. Since the horses weren't hard to make—a barrel or log, attached to a pair of rockers and fitted with some kind of head would do—most fathers could make one for their children. In the nineteenth century, industrialization lead to the mass production of more elaborate horses, and the models for wealthier children became larger and more realistic. By the mid-twentieth century, horses were being made of durable molded plastic, and several popular models were suspended on springs instead of mounted on rockers. Yet whether the mane was of horsehair or lengths of yarn, whether the saddle was "real" or imaginary, the horse was always loved and cherished, a toy that seemed to come alive to carry you, at lightning speed, to distant and exciting places.

VIEW-MASTER: Pop in a reel, flick the lever, and there you have it: your own private 3-D theater. View-master's roots go back to the stereopticons of the nineteenth century. The toy debuted in 1939, but got a real boost in 1951 when it bought a rival company, TruView. Not only did this put an end to costly competition, but opened the door to a gold mine: TruView had made a licensing agreement with the Walt Disney company to create products based on its movies and cartoon characters, and View-Master carried the relationship forward. Three-reel sets of movie tie-ins sent sales through the roof, and cemented its place as a children's favorite.

Make it an Old-Fashioned Candy Christmas

WISH 'EM THE BEST ... WITH

Brach's

Give three pounds of chocolate pleasure to those at the top of your list. BRACH'S CHRISTMAS CHOCOLATES

A lavish assortment of rich milk and dark chocolates, filled with such family favo~~as soft, smooth, full-flavored cremes, caramels, nougats, jellies and marmala~~An adventure in taste thrills. Luxuriously packaged. (Also available in 5 lb. b~~

~~Count on these colorful Christmas ~~candies to brighten your holidays . . . ~~BRACH'S BURGUNDY MIX

~~A sparkling assortment of cinnamon balls, rum-butter toffees, fruit slices, ~~utterscotch balls, crystal clear mints and filled hard candies in crisp-thin ~~avorful jackets—each piece wrapped in cellophane.

And all through the ho~~ . . . Keep brimming bowl~~ BRACH'S HARD CANDIES

Twenty Classic Stocking Stuffers

Oh, the joy of finding out what all those lumps and bulges were in the stocking hung with care! Here are some little toys that sweetened many a Christmas past.

ACTIVITY BOOKS: Who doesn't remember that sense of achievement in finding the way out of the maze, or counting all the monkeys in the tree? With a little box of activity books, a child could color, connect the dots, find the hidden picture, solve  puzzles, and stay busy for hours. Jazzier sets even included stickers, and in the days before peel-and-stick you had the added fun of the lingering taste of glue on your tongue.

BARREL OF MONKEYS: It seemed like a novelty toy that might last one or two years—little plastic monkeys, packaged in a plastic barrel, that challenged you to hook all twelve of them together. The thing was, children loved the toy, and the inexpensive novelty of 1965 became a classic.

BUBBLE SOAP: Soap was a big breakthrough for cleanliness-minded adults, but it was an even bigger breakthrough for children who love blowing bubbles. Soap is the perfect medium for creating transparent orbs swirling with reflected color. When toy manufacturers came up with no-fail formulas and sold the liquid with hoops, pipes, and even jazzier instruments, a classic was born.

CANDY CANES: Candy canes have been around since at least 1670, when sugar sticks were first distributed to children during a nativity ceremony at Germany's Cologne Cathedral. According to legend, their curved shape was created to resemble a shepherd's staff. The treat didn't go Technicolor until the beginning of the twentieth century, when red stripes and peppermint flavoring were added. In some ways, candy canes are the fruitcake of the Christmas stocking set. There are lots of better candies, and no one even seems to eat candy canes anymore, but somehow Christmas just wouldn't be the same without them.

CHANGEABLE CHARLIE: The perfect laptop toy, Changeable Charlie was a set of eleven blocks that fit neatly in a small box. Each block could be flipped to present a variation of a different facial feature. According to the box, the blocks made it possible to give Charlie 4,194,304 different expressions.

CRAYONS: The first box of Crayolas sold for a nickel in 1903. The scent of fresh, sharp crayons has been a part of Christmas ever since.

GUMBY: Gumby was created by Art Clokey and developed out of a 1955 short film called Gumbasia. The likeable green clay humanoid got a guest shot on Howdy Doody the next year and his own television show the year after. Unlike human stars, whose fame often burns out quickly, Gumby had staying power. He was soon joined by Pokey, his brick-colored horse, and both are still around.

KRAZY IKES: The brightly colored cylinders that could be snapped together to form whimsical animals and people have been around since the 1930s. Kits came with human heads  as well as animal ones, and bodies, arms, and legs that looked right on almost any creature you could dream up. Originally, the pieces were wood, but they were later made of plastic.

MAGIC SLATE: You owe it all to crime, that little toy made of waxed cardboard covered with a sheet of gray tissue and a sheet of clear film, which could be written on and magically erased simply by lifting the sheets. At least that's how the story goes. Back in the 1920s, just such a device was pitched to R. A. Watkins, who owned a small print shop in Illinois. He declined, but later that night received a call from the would-be salesman. He'd run afoul of the law, and offered the device again, this time in exchange for bail money. Watkins accepted, acquiring both domestic and international rights to the device.

MATCHBOX TOYS: One of the most successful British imports in history, tiny Matchbox cars, trucks, and tractors have been delighting American children since 1954. England's shop owners initially dismissed them as too small and inexpensive to appeal to children, but Woolworth stocked them and enjoyed brisk sales. What the toys lacked in size, they made up for in number and irresistible packaging, and soon parents worldwide got into the habit of watching where they walked.

MODELING CLAY: Long since replaced by Play-Doh, modeling clay was once the be-all and end-all for young sculptors. It came in a set of candy bar–sized colored slabs, usually with small wooden or rubber molds to make impressions with.

PEZ: The pelletlike Austrian candy, manufactured since the late 1920s, made its first appearance as an import in 1952. In 1955, the company introduced character dispensers. One of the first, Santa Claus, made the candy a particular hit at Christmas.

PLAY-DOH: Developed as a cleaning product for wallpaper, Play-Doh was first sold

as a toy in 1956, but didn't hit it big until 1957, when the original twenty-four-ounce can of off-white was divided into four smaller cans. Red, yellow, and blue were now added, and the toy became more

interesting to children. Fifteen years later, half a billion cans of the stuff had been sold. By the end of the century, the world was consuming Play-Doh at the rate of 2 ½ million cans a day.

PUZZLES: The first puzzle—a map—was invented as an educational tool in the mid-1700s, and has remained a favorite way of introducing children to shapes ever since. In the twentieth century, when a method was perfected for die-cutting a cardboard-backed picture, the jigsaw puzzle was born. Jigsaws were wildly popular in the 1920s—the more pieces and the more complex the better—and they became a traditional form of family entertainment, just right for long winter evenings spent indoors.

SILLY PUTTY: Thank World War II for this one. When rubber imports ceased for the duration, scientists across America got busy trying to concoct a synthetic form of the stuff. One of the failures was a substance that stretched and bounced, and flattened into a puddle when left alone. As an added bonus, when pressed onto newsprint, it picked up the print in amazing detail. It was useless as a rubber substitute but just great when it came to delighting children. Since 1950, more than three thousand tons of Silly Putty has been sold. It was even sent on the Apollo 8 mission—not as part of a scientific experiment, but on the sound theory that astronauts need toys, too.

Troll Toys . . . plus Mr. & Mrs. Mouse House

SLINKY: In 1945, after watching how a coiled spring behaved when it tumbled from his desk, Marine engineer Richard James told his wife, "I think I can make a toy out of this." Indeed he did, devising a spring that could "walk" down a flight of stairs. Gimbel's agreed to let James demonstrate the toy to Christmas shoppers, and all four hundred pieces sold in less than two hours. By Christmas of the next year, the toy James had named Slinky was available across America, and has been slithering its way into Christmas stockings ever since.

TROLL DOLLS: Just in time to pop out of stockings, the gleefully homely troll doll came along a few months before Christmas in 1963. The troll had been designed by a Danish woodcutter, Thomas Dam, in 1959 and was already popular in Europe. American manufacturers gave their own twist to the ugly urchin, replacing the original wool hair with wild, synthetic mops in colors like shocking pink and acid green. The Technicolor hair was just right for the American market, and articles in magazines such as *Time* and *Life* touting the troll's powers to confer good luck sealed the deal. The craze lasted into the mid-1960s, then seemed to vanish for a while. But almost every decade since has seen a return of the little doll that, for all its ugliness, brings a smile to everyone's face.

WHEE-LO: Since 1957, millions of children have been mesmerized by the little red wheel that seems to defy gravity by spinning along the inside and outside of a hand-held metal track. The secret: magnetic attraction.

WOOLY WILLY: Every one has had one at some time—a face printed on cardboard under a bubble of plastic filled with metal filings that could be moved with a magnetic wand to create features like beards, mustaches, and shaggy eyebrows on the face. The original was called Wooly Willy, and he and his kin have been delighting children since 1955.

YO-YO: The yo-yo had been around for a good hundred years by the time marketing expert Donald Duncan bought a small Los Angeles company that manufactured the toy. Duncan sent a fleet of "yo-yo men" to travel the country, demonstrating the toy and performing amazing tricks like "walk the dog" and "around the world." Boys especially loved the yo-yo, and saw mastery of one or more tricks as the height of cool.

SANTA'S SHOPPING LIST

Glass jeep or Army transport plane filled with candy, 1944: $.49

Krazy Ikes set with 56 pieces, 1944: $.77

Happi-Time magic slate, 1944: $.73

16-ounce box of modeling clay with four 4-ounce slabs of clay, each a different color, and 6 molds, 1947: $.44

Rocket bubble gun with soap, 1950: $.98

Magnetic Pick-Up Stix, 1951: $.67

78 RPM record, plastic, 1955: $.25

Wooly Willy, 1955: $.29

Whee-Lo, 1957: $.79

Play-Doh set, 4 6-oz. cans, 1958: $.66

Matchbox car, 1965: $.49

Troll doll, naked as the day he was born, 1966: $.66

Slinky, 1966: $.66

Gumby and Pokey, in their jeep, 1967: $2.99

View-Master 3-reel packs, 1967: $1.25